THE BOXERS OF WALES
Volume 3: Rhondda

Second Edition
(Expanded and Updated)

GARETH JONES

St David's Press
Cardiff

Published in Wales by St. David's Press, an imprint of

Ashley Drake Publishing Ltd
PO Box 733
Cardiff
CF14 7ZY

www.st-davids-press.wales

First Edition published – 2012
Paperback (978-1-902719-80-1)

Second (Expanded and Updated) Edition published – 2021
Paperback (978-1-902719-955)
eBook (978-1-902719-962)

© Ashley Drake Publishing Ltd 2021
Text © Gareth Jones 2021

The right of Gareth Jones to be identified as the author of this work has been asserted in accordance with the Copyright Design and Patents Act of 1988.

Every effort has been made to contact copyright holders. However, the publishers will be glad to rectify in future editions any inadvertent omissions brought to their attention.

Ashley Drake Publishing Ltd hereby exclude all liability to the extent permitted by law for any errors or omissions in this book and for any loss, damage or expense (whether direct or indirect) suffered by a third party relying on any information contained in this book.

All rights reserved. No part of this publication may be reproduced, stored in a retrieval system, or transmitted, in any form or by any means without the prior permission of the publishers.

British Library Cataloguing-in-Publication Data.
A CIP catalogue for this book is available from the British Library.

Typeset by Prepress Plus, India (www.prepressplus.in)
Cover designed by Books Council of Wales, Aberystwyth

CONTENTS

Acknowledgements	iv
Foreword	v
Introduction	vi

Najah ALI	1	Jack 'Shoni Engineer' JONES	74
Young ALLSOPP	3	Johnny JONES	76
Nobby BAKER	6	Percy JONES	78
Vernon BALL	9	Russell JONES	84
Young BECKETT	11	Sammy JONES	86
Tony BLACKBURN	13	Tommy JONES	89
Charlie BUNDY	15	Warren KENDALL	91
Gordon COOK	17	Mog MASON	93
Jerry DALEY	20	Colin MILES	96
Chris DAVIES	23	Billy MOORE	99
Les DAVIES	25	Rees MOORE	102
Kid DOYLE	27	Freddie MORGAN	104
Ivor DREW	31	Kelvin MORTIMER	108
Llew EDWARDS	33	Dave PETERS	110
Rhys EDWARDS	39	Lewis REES	113
Ralph EVANS	41	Terry REES	115
Wayne EVANS	43	Ken ROWLANDS	117
Tommy FARR	45	Neil SWAIN	119
Billy FRY	55	Tom THOMAS	123
Darron GRIFFITHS	58	Alun TREMBATH	130
Eddie JOHN	61	Kelvin WEBBER	132
Phineas JOHN	63	Jimmy WILDE	134
Barrie JONES	66	George WILLIAMS	148
Ginger JONES	68	Liam WILLIAMS	151
Harold JONES	71		

Supporting Cast	161
Bibliography	165

ACKNOWLEDGEMENTS

The more I seek help in putting together these books, the more willing hands come to my aid. Whether it is physical help – a lift here, the loan of a photo there – or simply the sharing of memories, their contributions have been vital.

Top of any list must come the boxers, whose achievements provide the skeleton of the enterprise. Those still, happily, with us have helped put flesh on those bones. The families of those for whom the final bell has tolled have been equally generous with background and anecdotes. But there are many others who deserve mention.

I am indebted to the legendary and much missed Cliff Morgan for contributing the foreword; to *Boxing News* and successive editors; to the British Boxing Board of Control, its general secretary Rob Smith and the staff at its Cardiff head office, along with Mark Warner, former secretary of the authority's Welsh Area Council; to John Waith, of the Welsh Amateur Boxing Association; and to the Welsh Ex-Boxers' Association and its officers, including Wynford Jones, Cyril Thomas and the sadly departed Dave Bethell, Johnny Jones and Don James.

I am grateful to the ever-helpful staff in the local studies departments of Cardiff, Pontypridd and Treorchy libraries.

And there are the individual enthusiasts, only too keen to pass on their knowledge: people like Dav Owens, Pete Bartlett, Dave Furnish, Huw Parry, Keith Willison, Howard Evans and Darren Pullman.

Special thanks go to the contributors to genealogical websites such as Rootschat, Rootsweb and the Great War Forum, in Britain, Australia and the US, who have given their time to help a stranger unravel some fistic family trees.

The book's illustrations have mostly been provided by those listed above, but I must also acknowledge the generosity of the professionals who have allowed me to use their work: Huw Evans Picture Agency (www. huwevansimages.com), Philip Sharkey, Ed Mulholland/Matchroom, Liam Hartery (www.liamhartery.com), Wayne Hankins and the late Les Clark, plus Menna James at the RCT Libraries.

My enthusiastic publisher, Rhondda-born Ashley Drake, also deserves my gratitude.

And, as ever, I pay tribute to the dedication of Harold Alderman, MBE, whose long hours spent poring over old newspapers have unearthed a wealth of information which he generously shares with lesser researchers like myself.

FOREWORD

I was born and bred in a valley where coal had created wealth and misery. In my youth the Rhondda sustained a community of hard-working men and women – a valley of pits and poverty, chapels and choirs. Sport was a precious part of a hard life, binding people together and forming great friendships.

I vividly remember, as a small boy, being taken by my parents to the middle of the field behind our house in Trebanog, where we, along with hundreds of others, gathered round the "Relay Shed" to listen to the radio commentary of that memorable fight when Tommy Farr challenged Joe Louis. My grandfather, Isaac Christmas Morgan, was actually in the States to see that epic event and never tired of talking about it.

Many years later, Tommy, great Welsh author Gwyn Thomas and I were in the Rex Cinema in Tonypandy to receive the Rhondda Awards trophy. Tommy told the audience of his pride in being a son of the valley and regaled them with tales of the joy of boxing. Gwyn responded drily, "It's wonderful to learn that Tommy has had so much fun in his life, for I've been told the only concession to gaiety in the Rhondda is a striped shroud!"

It was through a BBC radio sports programme, presented by G.V. Wynne-Jones, that I was privileged to meet the immortal Jimmy Wilde, who was very nervous beforehand. 'Geevers' told him, "Don't worry – I'll start by asking you where you had your first big fight and how much you were paid."

Then came the announcement: "Now, the greatest boxer at any weight in the world, 'The Ghost with a Hammer in his Hand', the one and only Jimmy Wilde!"

Jimmy ran on to the stage to thunderous applause and, before 'Geevers' could ask the question, grabbed the microphone and said, "Porth. Three and sixpence!"

I beg you turn these pages slowly and carefully, so that you can relish this wonderful tale of boxing and of the men from the Rhondda Valley who graced the ring over so many glorious years.

Cliff Morgan, CVO OBE

INTRODUCTION

The Rhondda, of all the South Wales valleys, is undoubtedly the best known. There are some in England and beyond who may well believe it is the only one; they would certainly struggle to name any others.

That fame did not come about by accident. In the fields of industry, politics, culture and sport, children of the Rhondda led the way. And, while rugby, football and cricket had their adherents, boxing was the sport which most stirred the blood of the locals.

It is no coincidence that the first two Welsh pugilists to wear that proud label "world champion" came from the Rhondda. But Percy Jones and Jimmy Wilde were just two of the fighting products of this combative community.

Tommy Farr, with his epic battle with the legendary Joe Louis, captured the imagination like none other between the wars.

And if the start of this millennium saw fewer practitioners come close to that sort of glory, Liam Williams has restored some lustre to its reputation. An impressive collection of belts might not include world honours, but his showing against Demetrius Andrade suggested they could yet arrive.

The locals' love of a good scrap was nurtured at, literally, the highest and lowest levels. Miners – and that meant the vast majority of the male inhabitants – would settle scores either in trenches cut in the pit floor, hundreds of feet below ground, or in the fresh morning air of the mountain top, out of sight of those authorities who would otherwise have intervened.

But once the introduction of gloves and the Queensberry Rules had made the sport at least semi-respectable, there was hardly a hall in the Rhondda (apart, obviously, from those belonging to the chapels) which did not host professional boxing, scarcely a pub which did not have a gym attached.

Most weekends between the wars would offer the fight fan a selection of venues, from Tynewydd and Maerdy down to Tonyrefail and Gilfach Goch. If there was no permanent structure suitable, the likes of Jack Scarrott and Joe Gess would set up tents on a local field.

This book will, I hope, honour some of those who thrilled the crowds back in the day, while also providing a reminder of a few more recent practitioners. To them all – and to those unnamed here who played their part in the Rhondda's fighting tradition – I offer my gratitude and respect.

GARETH JONES
June 2021

NAJAH ALI
(1980–)

- Commonwealth Super-Flyweight Challenger 2013
- Olympic Representative 2004

Few of the customers calling in at a Porth fast food joint were aware of it, but their kebab may well have been served up by a former Olympian. And one who was known around the world when he boxed in Athens in 2004.

Maybe his name is not as easily recognisable as that of Amir Khan, who won a silver medal at those Games, but Najah Ali earned his own headlines when he was plucked from war-torn Baghdad to wear the colours of the newly freed Iraq.

As part of their campaign to win the hearts and minds of the local populace, the US asked one-time world title challenger Maurice 'Termite' Watkins – he was actually in Iraq to help fumigate insect-ridden homes – to coach the national boxing team. Although none of the squad made it through the Olympic qualifying competitions, light-flyweight Ali, a gold medallist at the Asian Games of 2002, was awarded a wild card place by the International Olympic Committee.

Watkins took his new protégé to New York to prepare at the famous Gleason's Gym, while the American authorities made sure his story had widespread publicity, with Najah, unlike other athletes given similar assistance, ready to give interviews publicly supporting the US action, despite the risk of making himself a target for insurgents. All the more surprising, then, that after the Games, where he outpointed a North Korean before losing to former world bronze medallist Alexander Nalbandian, of Armenia, he was refused a visa to study in the US.

Najah Ali celebrates his winning Olympic bow

Ali, already a graduate in computer sciences, had been accepted for a course at Houston University, near the home of mentor Watkins, who had promised to pay for his tuition and accommodation. Three times Najah made the expensive and dangerous bus trip to Amman, in neighbouring Jordan, to apply at the American embassy. Each time in vain.

It was three years later that Frank Joseph, a London-based manager, persuaded him to come to Britain and turn pro and he spent a year living at Hanger Lane, while training with Johnny Eames at the TKO Gym. A first-round win in his debut boded well, but Ali disliked the constant rush of the metropolis and followed a friend's advice to move to Cardiff.

With former world champion Steve Robinson now in the corner, Ali followed up his first three wins by flooring unbeaten Michael Walsh at Wembley, only to run out of steam and be stopped in the third. Next up came the Mongolian-born Shinny Bayaar, who sneaked home by one point down the road from his adopted Lancashire home.

By now Ali had met and married a Rhondda girl, Kaylie Ann, and moved first to Clydach Vale and then to Porth. Training was now in the hands of Mark Hoban, a transplanted Geordie, at the Gelligaer gym used by new manager Dai Gardiner.

There was also progress in the ring. In September 2010 Najah caused a significant ripple in the domestic pond by outpointing former Commonwealth super-fly champion Don Broadhurst before his own Brummie supporters. The fairly meaningless International Masters bantam belt came as a bonus. Ali raised a few more eyebrows when he outpointed highly-touted Michael Maguire, a last-ditch knockdown clinching victory over the previously undefeated prospect.

By now a British citizen, Najah went to Liverpool Olympia and decked Ryan Farrag, a future European champion, en route to a points loss. He left a good enough impression that when a late replacement was needed to face Ellesmere Port's Paul Butler, Ali was called back to Merseyside on June 28, 2013, to challenge for Butler's Commonwealth super-fly belt.

The local took out his frustration on the substitute, dropping him in the opener and establishing early supremacy. Ali kept trying, but could rarely penetrate Paul's tight guard, and found himself vulnerable to an assault to the body that left him unable to beat the count when he was felled again in the fourth.

It also marked the end of his career, but not his connection with boxing. Now a father of three sons and working in a Cardiff call centre, Najah is also a coach in the revived Tiger Bay ABC in Butetown.

YOUNG ALLSOPP
(1901–1964)

🥊 Welsh Bantamweight Champion 1921–22

Back in the day, boxing people were pretty careless about names. Lads would appear in corners, with even the promoter barely interested in what they were called until they demonstrated it might be worth getting to know them better. "So-and-so's Nipper" or "Kid Whatsisname" were announced to the crowd, and reporters, if there were any, simply followed suit.

Spelling, too, was not something many bothered to check. Thus it was that William Jonathan Alsop became "Young Allsopp" when he first stepped into a ring. And they were still calling him that more than a decade later.

Jonty, as he was known at home, first saw the light of day in Rhys Street, Trealaw, the eldest child of a couple from the Bristol area who had moved to the Rhondda in search of work.

His early career was spent mainly on home soil, where he enjoyed enough success to be included in a tournament set up to discover Wales's top bantamweight. It was no easy task, given the depth of talent among little men in the area, but Allsopp outpointed Rhondda rival Harold Jones, useful prospect Silas Bunch and the experienced Caerphilly warrior, Arthur Bishop, to reach the final, where he would face Cardiffian Billy Davies, a former champion down at flyweight.

Young Allsopp

3

A miners' strike made major promotions unviable, forcing the pair to wait six months before they came together at the Cardiff Empire on October 22, 1921. Made over 20 rounds, it was the main event of a tournament to raise funds for a Mametz Ward at Cardiff Royal Infirmary – though the biggest draw was actually a mock bout between Jimmy Wilde and the comedian, George Robey.

Davies began well, using his educated left hand to advantage, although referee Jim Driscoll frequently admonished his fellow citizen (and, indeed, occasional sparmate) for claiming his man at close quarters, where Jonty was the more adept. Billy repeatedly protested about the Rhondda boy's illegal use of the head, but Allsopp's fists were also responsible for numerous marks on the Davies countenance. His mouth was bleeding from midway, his nose following suit in the 11th, seconds before he suffered a more significant injury.

The Cardiffian charged in recklessly, head down, and the resultant collision left him with a lengthy gash across the forehead. Allsopp was, by this time, in a clear points lead and Davies's seconds pulled him out, despite voluble protests from their charge. The new champion was presented with an ornate belt, amid generous applause from the loser's townsfolk.

Jonty had already made a few successful visits to Liverpool, but suffered a bad loss there at the start of 1922 against former British bantam king George McKenzie, the nephew of Jimmy Wilde's rival, Tancy Lee, when the towel was thrown in at the end of the third. He was never the same afterwards; he had gone ahead with the date despite being unable to spar because of an injured right hand.

But there was still huge interest when he came to defend his Welsh honour against Tylorstown's Albert Colcombe on May 20, 1922, at Llwynypia Baths, where the fans were "clinging to gas brackets". It was a cracking bout, starting with an exceptional display of close-quarter work from both men, although Albert's supremacy was underlined when referee W. Morgan warned Allsopp in the second and third for claiming his man. Jonty rocked Yorkshire-based Colcombe with a right early in the fourth and he was unsteady throughout the session, but the holder lacked the steadiness to finish the job.

After the escape, Albert switched tactics in the fifth, preferring to box behind a long left. The middle rounds were so closely fought that the

Jonty and his Welsh belt are immortalised in oils

Young Allsopp and his gym-mates at the Colliers Arms, Trealaw, in 1922. Jonty is seated fourth from the right in the second row. His trainer, Rees Henry, stands on the far left of the row behind.

referee twice halted proceedings to urge the crowd to control their emotions, but by the eighth Colcombe was well in command and the champion was shipping regular punishment. By the tenth, Allsopp's left eye was almost shut and, as his tormentor piled on the pressure, he eventually held out a hand in surrender, ending a brave showing.

Injuries sustained in a roof fall helped bring Jonty's career to a close and also left him unable to work underground. He sold his hard-earned belt to raise the cash to acquire a wholesale confectionery business, which later expanded into shops in Tonypandy and Rhoose, where he settled with his family. It was while working in the firm's warehouse that he suffered a fatal heart attack at the age of 63.

The family tradition has continued, with grandsons Anthony and Jonathan both wearing the Wales vest as amateurs, while Anthony's own sons also boxed, Adam claiming a Welsh youth title and Daniel twice becoming British Universities champion.

NOBBY BAKER
(1907–1978)

- Welsh Bantamweight Challenger 1927
- Welsh Lightweight Challenger 1930, 1935

They talk of three tries for a Welshman. But it doesn't always work out. The tough little miner from Trealaw had three cracks at a Welsh title, but finished second each time. No matter. He never needed a belt to become one of the most respected warriors of his generation.

Nobby Baker

The son of mountain fighter Walt, young Joseph – not that anyone knew him as that – first laced on the gloves at the local Colliers Arms when he was just 13, the same age he began at the Glamorgan Collieries in Llwynypia.

After a brief amateur career, the lad from Miskin Road quickly moved to cash in on his talent. And he was good enough to work his way to an early shot at the Welsh bantam king, Merthyr teenager Tosh Powell, whom he had previously outpointed. But when they met at Pontypridd on September 10, 1927, Baker was given a hiding, although he was still on his feet when the end came in the seventh round.

Perhaps weight-making played a part, as he easily outscored Powell in a rubber match – less than a month before Tosh suffered fatal injuries in a contest in Liverpool – and it was clear by then that Nobby's bantam days were behind him.

Nobby Baker (left) signs to fight the tragic Tosh Powell

In fact, it was as a lightweight that Baker had his next opportunity, taking on holder Gordon Cook on September 22, 1930, again at Pontypridd. Nobby was comprehensively outskilled, with the Penygraig man's southpaw stance proving a major problem. The two had been friends for years, but as rival factions argued over who was better, they did not speak for nine months before the fight; afterwards they were fine again and when Cook was taken ill Nobby was the first to volunteer his services for a benefit show.

One of the busiest fighters in Wales, he frequently boxed on consecutive nights at weekends, both at home and in the Midlands. There were sometimes as many as four outings a week – as well as his regular shifts underground.

He met everyone who was anyone in and around his weight division – he stopped London's wonder boy, Abercrave-born Nipper Pat Daly, and went the distance with British champions Johnny Cuthbert and Seaman Tommy Watson, though he was blown away inside a round by Olympic rep Harry Mizler – another who would wear the Lonsdale Belt – and that after Nobby's car broke down on the way to London.

The purse that night was just £8, but it was more than double what he earned in a week down the pit. And his readiness to don the gloves whenever the call came ensured regular additions to the Baker bank account.

Billy 'Ducks' Jones, the Cwmparc lad whose bout with Nobby turned into farce

But he still had his eyes set on a championship. When he overcame the bookies' odds to outpoint Vic Morris at Judge's Hall, it earned him the right to tackle Boyo Rees, by then wearing the lightweight strap, at the Mountain Ash Pavilion on October 14, 1935. It was an even match, with Boyo's left countered by Baker's right as each looked for power, with little regard for science. The champion's supremacy at close quarters put him in front going into the last third, before a left hook split Nobby's eyebrow in the 12th. Rees maintained his control to take a clear points decision.

It was far from the end for the Trealaw man, who figured in a bizarre bout in Bridgend against regular rival Billy 'Ducks' Jones (the nickname was in tribute to his elusive qualities) when the lights went out. The referee instructed the pair to walk around the ring until the gong, at which point they took their places on their stools. When the bell rang for the next, power had not returned, so the circumnavigation resumed until midway through the session, when the lights came back on and the duo began to throw punches again.

Baker faced another future star in Swansea prospect Ronnie James, who won in four. Even in 1946, at the age of 39, he renewed his Board licence, but any plans to prolong his career were ended when a roof fall at the Naval Collieries, Penygraig, damaged his spine and he spent many months in Porth Hospital, encased in plaster.

Doctors doubted he would ever walk normally, but he battled back and was able to return to the pit as a surface worker. A fund-raiser produced enough for Nobby to buy a grocery shop and newspaper business, but from then on his only connection with the fight game was to encourage son Ray in the amateur ranks.

VERNON BALL
(1924-2014)

 Welsh Lightweight Challenger 1948

When you are young, others make the big decisions for you. Parents, teachers – and boxing coaches – mull over what is best for you and come to their conclusions. It is not unusual for the subject of their deliberations to disagree. And such a reaction almost brought an early end to Vernon Ball's ring career.

Born in Smith Street, Gelli, he had taken up the sport at 10, learning the basics from Johnny Jones 'The Moel' at the Old Band Club in neighbouring Pentre. But Johnny refused to enter him for the Welsh schools championships, saying he was too small. Vernon took umbrage – and walked away from the gym for four years.

Just three days after his 14th birthday, he began work at the Lady Margaret colliery, Treherbert, soon moving to Fernhill, where he spent most of his mining life. But there was something nagging inside him and he eventually asked veteran trainer Ned Edwards to help him back into boxing.

He lost only three times in his first 15 bouts, including successful forays to the West of England. The run was ended at Cardiff Arms Park, when Vernon dropped a decision to debutant Ernie Davies, a pre-war Welsh amateur champion, and another star of the simon pures, future British and Empire king Cliff Curvis, also proved too good. Little Teddy Gardner travelled from Hartlepool to Porthcawl and took a 10-round verdict;

Vernon Ball

Gardner went on to win British, Empire and European flyweight belts, so there was no disgrace there.

By now, there had been changes beyond the ropes. Having set out without a recognised manager, Ball linked up with Tonyrefail-raised Billy 'Kid' Hughes, which saw the replacement of an unhappy Edwards by former Swansea Town footballer Billy Poole. Apart from a brief spell with Alf Lane in Treherbert, it was Poole in his corner for the next few years.

A draw with Welsh feather ruler Syd Worgan, following a knockout of former fly champion Dudley Lewis, earned Vernon an eliminator for the lightweight crown worn by Tonyrefail's Warren Kendall. The Gelli man saw off Ammanford's Reg Quinlan, but then came up short in a final eliminator against Jack Coles, from Tiryberth, despite scoring an early knockdown.

Ball regrouped, with a couple of victories over Tylorstown's useful Wally Downes among his successes. Soon Vernon was back in the title mix and a final eliminator decision over old rival Worgan clinched the opportunity.

Ball and Kendall met at the Gwyn Hall, Neath, on February 23, 1948, and Vernon gave it everything – indeed, it could be said he tried too hard, as his punches were notable more for their quantity than their quality. Kendall kept his cool, boxing more effectively, while also shaking his foe with occasional well timed rights, one of which dropped Ball for a brief count in the sixth. Things were always competitive, but it was the champion's arm raised at the end.

Vernon battled on, despite a split with trainer Poole, and was in contention for a crack at former victim Quinlan, who had dethroned Kendall. But a trip to Liverpool brought a one-sided pasting from Guyanese Allan Tanner, the referee calling a halt in the ninth, the first time for Ball to be stopped other than on cuts. When Londoner Tommy Burnham handed out similar treatment, closing both eyes and forcing Vernon to surrender after eight, it was enough. Still only 25, he announced his retirement.

Like so many others, he changed his mind, only to find that the Board would not renew his licence because of his poor eyesight. His optician testified that it was no worse than when he began, but, by his own admission, Vernon was never able to see his opponents until they came within range. The rejection saw him turn to the booths and other "unofficial" venues, his last fight coming when he was 42.

Beyond the ropes he had left the mines to work as a steel erector, a job he held for more than a quarter of a century before taking over a pub in Treherbert. He also played cricket, served Ton Pentre AFC as a committeeman, wrote an autobiography and became a leading light in the Welsh Ex-Boxers' Association.

YOUNG BECKETT
(1910–1972)

- Welsh Flyweight Challenger 1929

Young Beckett

It must be one of the most frustrating experiences in boxing. You work hard and earn a shot at a coveted belt. You give as good as you get against a respected champion. And the referee then declares the fight a draw.

And that feeling of "so near, yet so far" becomes so much worse when you never have a second chance to call yourself a champion. In Young Beckett's case, it was not for the want of trying.

Born William Alcwyn Williams, the Gelli lad was a bit of a prodigy. He won a Welsh schoolboy title when he was just 10, but that was only the half of it. He triumphed in the 7st 4lb division, despite weighing only 3st 6lb. A few pieces of lead sewn discreetly into his shorts concealed the disparity. At least, so goes the legend.

He was certainly considered one to watch when he turned pro under the guidance of former Welsh champion Johnny Jones 'The Moel' and top manager Teddy Lewis soon took an interest in his development. While still a teenager, he cut a swathe through rival flyweights at home and had already been introduced to audiences in London and Liverpool; in both cities he had become accustomed to the disappointment of drawn verdicts.

Beckett (left) spars with Cuthbert Taylor

At least that was better than when he visited the famous old Blackfriars Ring, won every round against Singapore fighter Bud Walley and saw ex-flyweight star Jim Kenrick walk to the other man's corner at the end. The *Boxing* reporter called the decision "weird and wonderful".

Two days before Christmas in 1929, the 19-yearold Gelli boy headed for Pontypridd's Palais de Danse to challenge Freddie Morgan for the Welsh championship. The holder, from Gilfach Goch, was two years older and making his first defence of the crown won at the same hall five months previously.

Beckett had himself to blame for the slow start which allowed Morgan to accumulate enough points to provide a cushion when the pace was stepped up in the later rounds. As Freddie tired, his early lead was wiped away, but, if the challenger's fast finish was sufficient to earn the nod in the minds of many ringsiders, it did not convince the man who mattered, referee Bob Hill. He lifted the arms of both men, allowing Morgan's reign to continue.

The lesson was clearly not learned. Just five days later, another lethargic opening required a late recovery from Beckett for another draw against Gwyn Thomas at Ammanford.

Perhaps he just did not care enough. There were repeated suggestions that he lacked ambition, happy to put on a show and entertain the public, rather than setting his mind on fulfilling his potential.

He did seek honours twice more. In the summer of 1934, now a featherweight and based in Shrewsbury, he faced Tirphil's George Morgan in Merthyr in a final eliminator for the Welsh nine-stone crown. Yet again his opponent took an early lead and this time, although Beckett boxed well on the retreat and finished strongly, he was unable to claw back the deficit.

A few months later he was matched in another eliminator against Morriston's Danny Thomas, a points victory earning him a crack at Maesteg man Stan Jehu, with the winner to challenge new ruler Morgan. Jehu, who had been dethroned by George, outworked the more skilful Beckett and went on to regain his throne.

For the Gelli man, there were a few more years as a journeyman, but soon after the outbreak of war his career drifted to a close.

TONY BLACKBURN
(1955–)

● Welsh Heavyweight Challenger 1976

Boxing at the National Sporting Club may not have carried the kudos in the 1970s that it did in the early years of the century, when boxing was run from that organisation's original Covent Garden home. But it was still something for a working-class boy from Tonyrefail to become a favourite of the dinner-jacketed toffs as they smoked their post-prandial cigars beneath the chandeliers of the Café Royal.

And the young redhead from Penrhiwfer Road appeared no fewer than 18 times within those august portals in Piccadilly, more than half the bouts in a four-year pro career.

Allan Blackburn – the 'Tony' came from the Radio One DJ – first boxed at 12 in the gym at the old Ely pub in Thomastown, but when that shut trainer Albert Cox took his boys to the Penygraig home of Rhondda ABC and it was in their colours that the youngster captured a British junior title – winning the final inside a round – before following up with a Welsh ABA championship at light-heavyweight

A few weeks past his 18th birthday, Blackburn signed up with mentor Cox, making his paid bow with a points success in Cardiff, but a month later he was strutting his stuff before the patrons of the NSC and was soon back to begin a run of a dozen consecutive contests there, losing just twice.

Tony now found himself meeting a better standard of foe and his record

Tony Blackburn

suffered accordingly. Useful Londoner Tony Moore outscored him twice, while unbeaten John L. Gardner was given a similar decision at the Albert Hall, though the half-point margin in favour of the future British champion was roundly booed. Gardner was more than half a stone heavier, too, with Blackburn well inside today's cruiserweight limit.

The odd success still came Tony's way, but defeat in five rounds by Reading puncher Les Stevens began the final decline. Ironically, it was only now that the Tonyrefail plant fitter had his shot at the vacant Welsh heavyweight crown at Swansea's Top Rank Suite on March 29, 1976.

Jamaican-born Neville Meade had settled in Wales's second city on turning pro with local businessman Eddie Richards, who promoted the title bout just three weeks after his charge had been outpointed in Spain by Alfredo Evangelista, later to go the distance with Muhammad Ali.

Despite the short turnaround, Neville imposed himself from the opening bell, using his reach advantage to control matters against a man with whom he had often shared the sparring ring.

Meade's vaunted power came into play in the fourth, a big right sending Blackburn sprawling, and when he rose at eight, still groggy, another right was awaiting him. Somehow Tony stayed upright, trying to get inside and hold, but Neville staggered him with an uppercut and referee Adrian Morgan stepped in after two minutes of the session. There were no complaints from the loser.

There was, in truth, little left. Another two stoppages, at the hands of Yorkshire duo Steve Carr and Neil Malpass, were enough for Blackburn to realise it was time to hang up the gloves.

After a career with the electricity board, Allan – to revert to his out-of-ring name – became one of the first police community support officers when they were introduced in 2003. And he also went back to his first love, setting up Tonyrefail ABC in 2011 with former PC Gary Davies.

CHARLIE BUNDY
(1912–2000)

- Welsh Light-Heavyweight Challenger 1934
- Welsh Heavyweight Challenger 1935

It would be unimaginable today, when most title contenders are full-time boxers able to devote weeks, even months, to preparing for their big chance. Even those who still cling to day jobs usually have sponsorship to cover time off for training when a fight is on the horizon.

But when Charlie Bundy was named to challenge the great Tommy Farr for the Welsh light-heavyweight crown on September 14, 1934, it was very different. So the Cwmparc man worked a full, back-breaking shift down the local pit, went home for a bath and then walked all the way to the Judge's Hall in Trealaw.

Despite his exertions, Bundy surprised the hot favourite with his performance, giving Farr problems throughout the 15 rounds. In the ninth he hurt Tommy with a series of body shots, but the holder survived, regained his composure and finished a convincing winner. Charlie then walked home to Cwmparc.

The very fact that he was in with Farr raised a few eyebrows. Not only had he lost twice before to the Clydach Vale man, he had been outpointed in a final eliminator by the former ruler, Randy Jones, whose height and reach advantages proved decisive.

Not that Charlie, one of 11 children, ever harboured doubts about his right to mix in such company. One of Jack Petersen's main sparring partners, he was said to be "the personification of confidence".

Charlie Bundy

Charlie (left) with British champion Jack Petersen

A motorcycle crash sidelined him for a few months and, when he returned, it was as a heavyweight. He was soon picking up the biggest purse of his career – a whopping £50 – for facing British light-heavy champion Eddie Phillips in a non-title outing at the Welsh White City in Cardiff's Sloper Road. It was only a late rally by the laidback Londoner, who could boast three wins over Farr, that earned him a draw, even though Charlie was handicapped by a closing left eye and an arm injury and finished totally exhausted.

A month later, on June 8, 1935, Bundy met Big Jim Wilde at the Mannesmann Hall in the latter's home town, Swansea, for the Welsh heavyweight throne vacated by Petersen. The taller Wilde kept Bundy at a distance throughout, never letting him get inside. Charlie did make Jim miss regularly, but his own blows lacked the crispness of his opponent's and there was little doubt about the verdict.

That was as close as Bundy came to a title, though he continued boxing for another 10 years. And he did cross gloves with other champions: Jack London, father of Brian, who knocked him out in three, and Bruce Woodcock, who climbed off the deck to outpoint him, both went on to occupy the British heavyweight throne.

A miner all his life, apart from a brief spell as a grocer, Charlie settled after the war in Llanharan, where he was still residing at his death, shortly after his 88th birthday.

GORDON COOK
(1905-1978)

🥊 Welsh Lightweight Champion 1928–29, 1930–31

When the fairground tough guys challenged the greying figure in Sam McKeowen's booth, they must have thought he was easy meat. When he then removed a glass eye and handed it to the timekeeper to look after, their confidence no doubt soared. Things changed when the bell rang.

By rights, Gordon Cook should not have been in the ring at all. But, having given up the sport on medical advice, it was similar counsel that prompted him to return. The first doctor, noting that his eyesight was deteriorating dramatically, persuaded him to retire at just 26, handing back his Welsh lightweight belt. Almost two decades later, a second, worried by his bronchial cough, urged Gordon to find work in the fresh air. A boxing booth was probably not what he had in mind.

The story began in Station Street, Penygraig, where the young Gordon Cooke – the final 'e' fell off somewhere along the way – was raised. Collier father Archie did a bit with his fists and his third son inherited his passion. By the time he was 15, he was already bringing in a few bob from boxing to help with the hard-pressed family budget.

Starting as a flyweight under the tuition of Rees Henry, the young southpaw

Gordon Cook

added poundage and experience until, as he emerged from his teens, he was collecting wins over significant rivals such as Charlie Stone, Haydn Williams and Evan Williams, which moved him into Welsh title contention.

The deal was clinched when Cook won a youth-versus-experience battle at Llwynypia Baths, cutting and outscoring Billy Fry to deliver the first loss of the Penygraig veteran's comeback. The bout occurred just as the new Welsh Board named four men to box an eliminating series for the right to challenge lightweight king Edgar Evans. Fry and Cook had been matched separately, but Gordon's success clearly satisfied the authorities and they sanctioned a straight shot, which took place at the Palace Theatre, Crumlin, on July 30, 1928.

The outcome was so convincing that there was no murmur of dissent from Evans's hometown fans when referee C.B. Thomas raised the Rhondda man's arm after 20 rounds. Cook's speedier footwork and crisper punching proved decisive, with the ageing Evans slow by comparison. Edgar kept battling, but could never manoeuvre Gordon into a position that allowed him to land more than single shots in a gruelling, if not particularly exciting contest.

Cook's first defence saw him face West Wales champion Arthur Davies two months later in front of a packed house at Brackla Hall, Bridgend. The Ammanford-based challenger could not cope with the holder's wrong-way-round style, but cut Gordon's eye in the fourth, only to suffer a gash of his own two rounds later. The Rhondda man walked on to a right in the 12th and looked in trouble, but recovered his senses to take a clear-cut verdict.

It was not until July 27, 1929, that Cook again put his title on the line, facing London-based Haydn Williams, originally from Blaengwynfi, again at the Brackla, where hundreds were turned away. Gordon lacked his usual aggression and, seemingly, self-belief. In the event, Williams himself was far from his best, but beat the champion to the punch for most of the bout. Cook, who may have had trouble weight-making, had little sting in his blows, although he did hand out a flash knockdown with a right in the fifth and C.B. Thomas's verdict against him was not universally welcomed.

But Gordon was far from finished. When Williams was stripped for refusing to defend, Cook was matched with Ashton Jones, a former gym-mate and long-time friend, at Trealaw's Judge's Hall on January 31, 1930, to fill the vacancy. The biggest bout in the Rhondda for a decade, it lived up to expectations.

The rangy Cook, showing superb ring generalship, took the initiative from start to finish, his southpaw right constantly in Jones's face. Local boy Ashton made a desperate effort to save the day with an all-out attack in the 11th, but the Penygraig man – though soon to move to Cardiff – had the defensive skills to survive, despite an early cut. Nine days later Cook removed all doubts about his legitimacy by outscoring former champion Williams at his new home, the Alcazar, Edmonton.

His second reign saw only one defence, a comfortable outing in which he outclassed the game Nobby Baker in Pontypridd, before failing eyesight began to become a problem. By June 1931 it was so bad that he was forced to retire, handing back his title.

There was a brief attempt at a return the following year, but Cook eventually accepted reality and relocated to Bournemouth, where he worked in an electroplating factory, though maintaining his connection with boxing assisting in the corner at many of the early fights of local boy Freddie Mills, later to become a world champion and showbiz star. He even became a referee – evidently, the fact that he was now totally blind in one eye was no obstacle!

When the factory fumes began to affect his lungs, Gordon made his "comeback" on the booths, earning enough money in one summer to buy a smallholding, where he grew vegetables and raised pigs, while enjoying a regular flutter on the horses.

But he still couldn't settle. He, wife Hilda and their son, Raymond, emigrated to California, where he died in San Francisco at the age of 73.

JERRY DALEY
(1908–1954)

- Welsh Middleweight Champion 1930–32

Jerry Daley

Wherever they went on the planet, the Irish took with them the love of a good scrap. Many of the ring's outstanding performers have roots in the Emerald Isle and that applied as much in Wales as anywhere. One such was Jeremiah Daly.

Father Patrick crossed the water from Bantry, moving around South Wales in search of work. In Merthyr he found a wife, Ellen. While they were living in Cardiff's Adam Street, young Jerry was born. Two years later the family were in Trebanog and it was in the Rhondda that the boy learned to box.

His education was in the hands of Billy Moore, still an active campaigner himself, but now with a gym at his disposal, having taken over as licensee of the Gethin Hotel in Penygraig. Young Daley – an 'e' had somehow infiltrated his surname – flourished under his guidance and was soon competing with the best local middleweights.

When Jerry went to Ammanford and outpointed Welsh champion Billy Green, it prompted the Taffs Well fighter to relinquish the belt. The Board matched Jerry with Glen Moody, from the Pontypridd fighting family, to decide his successor.

The fans at Judge's Hall, Trealaw, on February 14, 1930, saw one of the best fights between big men in Wales for many a day. Daley had the greater stamina and was the heavier puncher, but it was only from the 13th round that he surged ahead. The Ponty man faded and his left eye was swollen shut for the last three sessions, following a thumping right hand. Glen's crisper punching had seen him ahead until the ninth, but once Jerry stepped up the pace, landing heavy swings and uppercuts, he was forced to hold and attempt to spoil more frequently.

Daley was to wear the crown for more than two years, seeing off four challengers. First up, at Pontypridd, was Maesteg's Trevor Evans, who was on the defensive throughout, apart from occasional vain attempts to get inside. Jerry was happy to coast his way to a decision in a less than enthralling encounter.

Stoker Taff Howard, a naval man from Abercwmboi, had his opportunity at Swansea's Shaftesbury Theatre, but he was

The deal is done between Daley (rt) and Glen Moody

so out of condition that, after he was despatched in three rounds, promoter Dai Curvis (father of Cliff and Brian) withheld his purse.

A defence against Ynysddu's Young Anth – real name Anthony Morgan – attracted a huge crowd to Blackwood Skating Rink and, although Daley wasted a lot of energy battering away at the challenger's tight defence, Anth was wild in attack and earned referee Bill Allen's disapproval by repeatedly holding and hitting. Jerry kept his belt with a clear points verdict.

A trip through the Severn Tunnel to Bristol saw Daley battered by British and Empire middle boss Len Harvey in a non-title encounter. The towel was thrown in after three rounds and Daley berated his seconds, his gameness impressing Harvey, who visited his dressing-room to offer Jerry work in Windsor as his chief sparring partner. Jack Petersen also regularly employed him in that role.

Daley's fourth defence came against an old rival, Dai Beynon, in Ystradgynlais, promoted by a precocious 21-year-old, Elvet Davies. The Merthyr man was on the receiving end throughout, the bell saving him in the fifth, before a perfect right in the ninth left him lying beneath the ropes, his head hanging over the apron. After four seconds a cornerman pushed him back into the ring and referee Bill Allen halted the count and announced a disqualification, robbing Jerry of a knockout.

The Penygraig man's record-breaking reign – nobody else had made four successful defences – came to an end at the familiar hands of Moody in

Ammanford on March 28, 1932. Daley forced the pace for the first six rounds, but Glen began to land uppercuts in the seventh and the pattern of the fight changed. Jerry briefly rocked his challenger in the 12th, but it was an isolated gesture.

A year later Daley was given a crack at the vacant Welsh light-heavy crown, but gave almost a stone away to West Walian Randy Jones at Merthyr on March 11, 1933, and a cut near his right eye from the fourth did nothing to help. Daley focussed on the body, but was generally outboxed by the more skilful Jones.

A points defeat by the fast-rising Tommy Farr – the pair had previously drawn – underlined that Daley was on the slide. Injuries were proving harder to shake off: as well as damage to hands and a shoulder which prompted retirement in two 1933 bouts, there was a hernia sustained when he stumbled while carrying his bedridden father. Eventually, following medical advice, Jerry hung up his gloves.

He opened a boxing school at the Black Diamond Hotel, Edmundstown, and later at the Dunraven Hotel, Tonypandy, before moving to Bath to work on the railways, although he soon had a gym up and running there as well.

His choice of employment proved tragic, however. In April 1954, he died after being struck by a passing train. The Rhondda-Irishman was only 45.

CHRIS DAVIES
(1974–)

- Commonwealth Light-Heavyweight Challenger 2001
- European Junior Bronze Medallist 1992

The Mountbatten Leisure Centre in Portsmouth can be an intimidating place. Particularly when the Pompey football fans are there, prominently featuring the bare-chested, multi-tattooed characters once familiar to viewers of *Match of the Day*. And they always came out in force to support local hero Tony Oakey.

This was the scenario which faced a Rhondda factory worker on October 20, 2001, when he challenged the unbeaten Oakey for the Commonwealth light-heavy belt Tony had acquired five months earlier. Not that the prospect fazed 27-year-old Davies, despite the fact that he had come in as a late replacement for injured British champion Neil Simpson, a ringside observer.

Indeed, Chris started confidently, hooking to the head and taking the first three sessions, with the stocky holder struggling to land his trademark uppercut. The Welshman's switch-hitting posed a further problem, though Oakey seemed to find things easier when the challenger tried the southpaw stance.

Yet it was while "the wrong way round" that Davies hurt Tony with a jolting right in the fourth, but the Havant man's renowned chin stood the test and his equally respected stamina saw him gradually exert control over the exchanges. Blood poured from Oakey's nose, but he maintained a high pace and a greater workrate, which may have proved decisive in the final analysis.

Referee Dave Parris paused briefly at the final bell before turning to Oakey and lifting his hand amid tumultuous celebrations. Neither Davies

Chris Davies

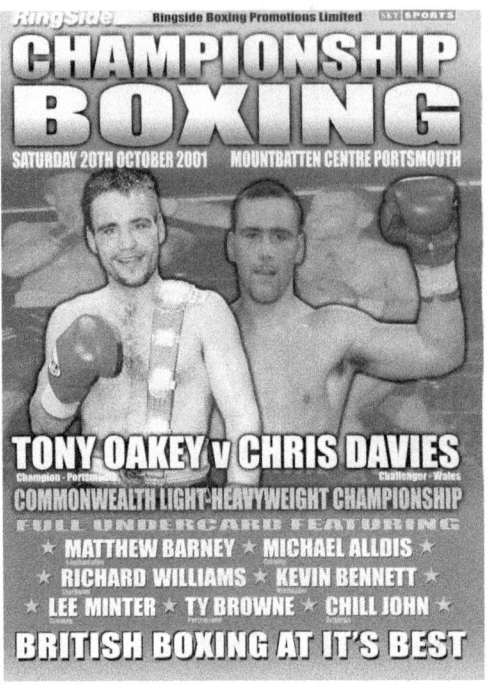

So close to a title – Chris v Tony Oakey

nor his small band of supporters risked any public show of dissent, despite their disappointment.

Privately, they felt robbed. Several of Oakey's more domesticated backers, including his brother, sympathised with that assessment, while *Boxing News* editor Claude Abrams was among the neutrals who had Davies ahead. But, in fairness, many rounds could have gone either way. And there is no suggestion that Mr Parris, himself a former pro heavyweight, was in any way influenced by the fearsome mob surrounding the ring in giving his 116–114 vote to the home fighter.

It was the best performance of Davies's career, yet he boxed only twice more – both wins – before giving up the logistical battle to combine training with shift work at the Sunjuice plant at Llantrisant.

The boy from Blaenclydach first attracted attention with a clutch of Welsh age-group titles in the colours of the Rhondda ABC, with the highlight of his amateur days a bronze medal at the European Junior Championships in Edinburgh in 1992, losing 8–7 to Turk Sinan Samil Sam, later to rule over Europe's pro heavyweights – after having three points deducted for slapping.

Davies was still a teenager when he turned pro with manager Dai Gardiner. He found it tough, losing four of his first six contests – one on cuts against future WBC champion Glenn Catley – before getting his act together and winning seven of his next eight, the only setback coming on points in Spain.

A two-round demolition of former British middle king Neville Brown and an even quicker victory over highly touted Irishman Cathal O'Grady propelled Chris into title contention, but he was worn down in eight rounds by London-based Nigerian Peter Oboh in a Commonwealth eliminator. It merely delayed his shot at the belt, but Oakey – and that crowd – proved too much.

After a spell focusing on rugby, as a trophy-winning coach with Wattstown and Cambrian Welfare, Davies returned to boxing, training youngsters and also providing security at both pro and amateur shows.

LES DAVIES
(1962–)

- Welsh Cruiserweight Challenger 1986

When you have beaten someone in the amateur ranks, you can be forgiven for expecting a repeat performance if fate throws you together again among the professionals. But it doesn't always work out that way. And the reverse was so emphatic that it brought a premature end to the Cymmer carpenter's career.

Les Davies, originally from Pontygwaith, first came up against Abner Blackstock when an amateur with the Gilfach Goch club. It was at the Rhondda Leisure Centre, Ystrad, in a heavyweight prelim of the 1983 Welsh ABA championships. Blackstock, representing Newport's Phoenix ABC, had won the light-heavy title the previous year – and would do again the following season.

Les Davies and his nephew, double Welsh ABA champion Lloyd Davies

But he proved no problem for the ambitious Davies, who romped to a points win and then saw off Cardiff teenager John Farrugia before facing Alan Price, a former Marine from Fishguard, in the final at the STAR Leisure Centre.

All looked straightforward when he forced Price to take a standing eight count in the opener. The West Walian battled back in a toe-to-toe tussle, but Davies finished strongly to clinch the crown via a majority decision.

Pembrokeshire bus driver Price popped up in the opposite corner when Les made his paid bow in 1985 after signing with manager Dai Gardiner. There was no problem as the new boy belaboured Alan's midriff to such effect that referee Adrian Morgan called a ceasefire in the second.

But next up was that man Blackstock. This time it was the Jamaican-born machinist having his first taste of the pro game and he rocked Davies's blond head back with an uppercut on the way to a close points victory. Injury sidelined Les for a while and he was carrying a few surplus pounds when he returned to stop Hull's Terry Gilbey in five, again thanks to his favoured body shots.

There was little time to celebrate. Blackstock was waiting. The pair were matched in the first-ever contest for the Welsh cruiserweight title, staged at Risca Leisure Centre on May 23, 1986, and Abner, with advantages in height, reach and mobility, chose that evening to reach a level he never again approached.

He buzzed around Davies like a bluebottle, firing in blows from unpredictable angles, switching stances and landing almost at will. Les's preparation had been disrupted by the death of mentor Ken McCann's mother and he was well below par. At times it seemed as if the Rhondda fighter was being surrounded – by one man!

In the ninth he hurled himself forward in desperation, only to be deposited in the ropes by Blackstock's right counter; when he was wobbled again seconds later, referee Ivor Bassett had seen enough. Davies was still wearing a bewildered expression an hour later.

It was a loss so comprehensive that Les never boxed again. But he is still involved on the training side, having set up Tylorstown ABC in 2010, and has helped guide nephew Lloyd Davies to two Welsh ABA titles.

KID DOYLE
(1893–1982)

- Northern Welterweight Champion 1915, 1916
- Welsh Welterweight Challenger 1919

Much about Kid Doyle was not what it seemed. For starters, his name was not Doyle. Although frequently billed as the Welsh welterweight champion, he never held the title. And, in the 1960s, he was reported as having lived in Llwynypia for 40 years, whereas, in fact, he had emigrated to the US in 1922.

The story starts in Hastings, where Cyril Martin Munnery was born. But he soon found himself in an orphanage; they told him his parents had died in a train crash. He was sent to stay with a Kent farm wagoner called Samuel Austen, taking his surname (though spelling it Austin), but moved in his teens to stay with a family named Pigford and work in the Durham coalfield, where he was known as Cyril Pigford. Keeping up so far?

While there he visited a booth with a couple of friends and boxed a trial. He did well enough to be invited to turn pro, at which point he adopted the handle by which fight fans would know him for the next dozen years.

A year after he married Geordie girl Alice Price war broke out and the youngster joined the Royal Field Artillery,

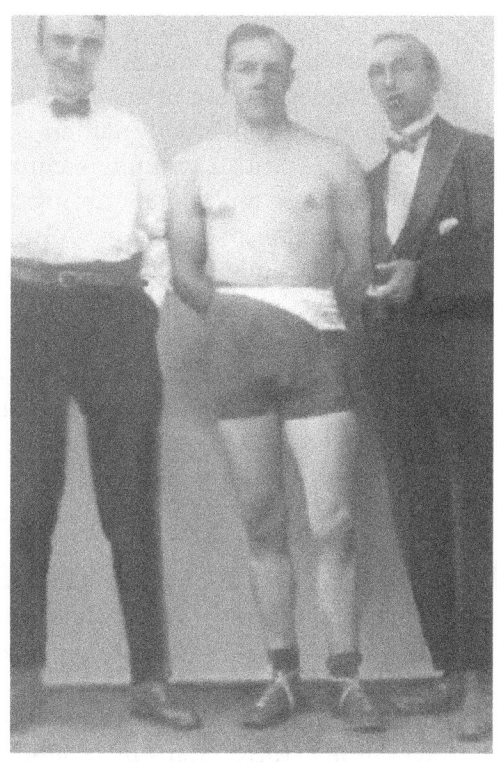

Kid Doyle, with trainer Dai Thomas (left) and backer Tommy Brice

The young marrieds – Kid and Alice in 1922

only to be discharged a month later when they discovered a problem with his eyes. It was not enough to prevent him boxing, however, and he continued to build a solid reputation on Tyneside.

Invitations began to arrive from further afield and Doyle became a regular at the famous Liverpool Stadium. His second visit saw him outpoint former two-weight British champion Johnny Summers and the all-powerful National Sporting Club took note, offering the Kid a title shot if he could do it again at their home in Covent Garden. But that went on the back burner when Doyle suffered a couple of setbacks against big-punching Swiss Albert Badoud and Scottish welter king Eddie Beattie.

The Glaswegian, who had been beaten on home ground in a scrap with the Northern title at stake, travelled south three months later, seeking revenge. In a tremendous battle, Beattie looked out on his feet at the end of the 10th, but dropped Doyle with a desperate right at the start of the next. He staggered up, grabbed Beattie and both crashed to the deck. Eddie rose first and when the Kid followed, the Scot floored him again and the count was interrupted by the towel floating in.

Late in 1915, Doyle headed for Tonypandy to work underground, but his first meeting with a Welsh rival was on familiar territory in Liverpool, where he lost a tight points decision in a non-title bout with British ruler Johnny Basham.

By the time the long awaited NSC clash with Summers was finally sorted, it was little surprise that the Londoner knocked the Kid out with a body punch in the second; he repeated the feat in Liverpool, though it took 14 rounds longer.

Still a favourite at the stadium in Pudsey Street, Doyle outpointed old foe Beattie to reclaim the Northern honour, but he was building a substantial following in his new community, who were not best pleased when Welsh rugby international Jerry Shea was adjudged the winner after 15 rounds at Llwynypia Baths. One fan threw a chair at the referee, who then escaped the building dressed as a policeman.

Doyle then finished strongly to outpoint future British middle and light-heavy champion Frank Moody, at the same venue, on October 21, 1918, in what some insisted was for the Welsh welter title, though such rules as existed did not allow for residential qualification.

A return with Basham was announced as "for sidestake and purse", with no mention of Johnny's Lonsdale Belt being up for grabs, although both weighed inside the welter limit. The Newport man was down in the second, doing a complete somersault, but recovered to survive the session, boxing well at close quarters to earn a decision which was well received outside a pocket of Doyle fans.

When the Kid was matched with old rival Shea at Mountain Ash Pavilion on July 26, 1919, local and national newspapers agreed that it was for the Welsh welter championship, though none of the reports suggested that Doyle was defending the honour. At the end nobody was the wiser. Despite flooring the recently capped Newport centre twice, the Kid had to settle for a draw. There had been pre-fight talk of the winner fighting American Augie Ratner, who had been in Britain for six months, but neither ever did.

Still together after 60 years

Two months later another draw, with Aberavon's Will Brooks, left the situation no clearer, but it was fairly academic as Doyle never boxed in Wales again. When the great Ted 'Kid' Lewis stopped him twice inside a month, it was effectively the end.

Doyle, who had invested his ring earnings in a mining level at Llwynypia, was involved in a similar venture in the Forest of Dean, moving to Yorkley, where he promoted himself in a three-round victory over old stablemate Jim Jenkins.

But when trainer D.J. Thomas, alias 'Dai Bandage', left Penygraig to become a fruit farmer in the US, Doyle, who already had relatives there, took the same route, buying a small mine in Illinois. He had a couple of fights, but, when his business fell foul of local union restrictions, Cyril Austin, as he was again known, had to focus on earning a living in someone else's pit.

He and Alice settled in the small town of Decatur, raising two children, and had been married for nearly 70 years when the one-time Kid died in 1982.

IVOR DREW
(1913–1983)

- Welsh Lightweight Challenger 1936

Howard Winstone is not the only Welsh fighter to have carved out a career in the ring despite having one of his weapons blunted by an accident at work. Ivor Drew lost the tips of three fingers on his right hand in a mishap down the pit, but the youngster from Trealaw did not allow it to hold him back.

First lacing on the gloves as a 10-year-old and learning his trade in the booths, he was still a teenager when he turned pro under the guidance of Fred Jenkins, proprietor of the Lusitania Fish Saloon in Penygraig, where he supervised two types of battering.

Ivor made steady progress and victories over the likes of Mog Mason, Jerry O'Neil and Cuthbert Taylor helped earn him recognition as a "Promising Provincial" in the trade magazine, *Boxing*.

Although there were occasional visits to exotic places like Belfast and Southport, Drew rarely ventured beyond the Valleys and it was on home ground at the Judge's Hall that he faced Evan Morris in an eliminator for the Welsh feather crown. The pair had met before, when Ivor, then barely more than a flyweight, outboxed Morris before his own Pontycymmer supporters. But this time, something went wrong.

Instead of relying on his extra height and reach, the local man opted to slug it out with a slugger. He allowed Evan to force the pace,

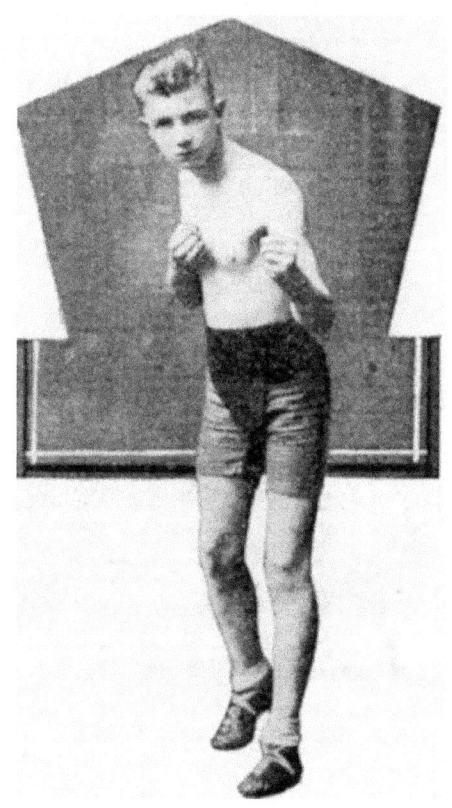

Ivor Drew

content to lie on the ropes and cover up, as if expecting the visitor to punch himself out. It never happened and, despite being clearly the better boxer, Drew was staggered by a right at the end of the tenth and needed the bell to save him. When he was again driven back in the 12th, Ivor's head slipped beneath the top rope, but, to the recipient's surprise, Morris continued to fire in shots at his defenceless victim.

When the referee leapt between them, some thought it was to disqualify the Garw Valley man. Not so. It was to raise Evan's hand in victory. But if controversy surrounded the ending, it was Ivor's own mistaken tactics which cost him the fight.

Three years later, up at lightweight, Drew finally had his title shot, following a run of success in which his 'W' column included Doug Kestrell, Nobby Baker and Young Beckett. Once again he was at home in Trealaw when he took on holder Boyo Rees on April 17, 1936. And once again, in an important contest, he had the physical advantages.

But the stocky champion from Abercwmboi brushed aside Ivor's leads, getting in close to work the body to good effect. His aggression impressed the referee enough to secure the verdict, although there were plenty of good judges at the Judge's Hall who thought Drew was hard done by.

The Rhondda boy had little time to consider what might have been. Within a month he was knocked out inside a round by Midlander Len Wickwar, with defeats against Scouse duo Nel Tarleton and Peter Banasko underlining his place on the wider scene. Domestically, Ivor was still holding his own, but when he began to lose to those he had previously beaten, his enthusiasm began to wane.

With times hard in his homeland, Drew upped sticks and settled in Leicester, ironically the home town of conqueror Wickwar, where he married his Tonyrefail-born girlfriend, Novidia, and raised two sons.

The war saw him serve as a PTI in the Royal Artillery Regiment, before heading for Karachi as a military policeman. He put on the gloves once more and was crowned lightweight champion of North-West India, but was never tempted to resume his career when back in civvy street.

LLEW EDWARDS
(1892–1965)

- British Featherweight Champion 1915–16
- Empire Featherweight Champion 1915–16
- Australian Lightweight Champion 1916–19

Like most of the lads at the Cymmer Collieries, young Llew Edwards headed for the gym after work. But while the others eagerly pulled on the boxing gloves for impromptu sparring sessions, for Llew they held no attraction. Then he had an argument below ground.

An exchange of words led Edwards to give another lad a clip around the ear, which prompted the familiar response: "My big brother will get you."

When said elder sibling turned up a few days later, he was at least two stone heavier. He grabbed Llew around the neck and gave him a real going-over with the other hand. Forced to miss a few days' work to recover, Edwards was determined he would never again get involved in a fight.

But his workmates insisted that he had to stand up for himself and challenge the brother to meet him in the ring, where he would not be allowed to use the headlock. The reluctant Edwards was persuaded – and when the rematch took place, Llew sparked him with one punch.

That, for the victor, was that. But he was now a hero to his friends, who entered him for a local tournament. When he demurred, they accused him of being scared. So he went through with it. And won. There was now no turning back, especially when he realised he could earn a few bob.

Llew Edwards

Llew (left) with mentor Jim Driscoll

It was an unlikely career choice for someone who had happily allowed his more combative kid brother to sort out his problems as he grew up on a farm near the tiny Shropshire village of Llynclys, in the Welsh-speaking enclave around Oswestry. Hiram Llewellyn Edwards was just five when his quarryman father died and, with his mother scraping a living as a charlady, there was pressure on her 10 children to contribute to the family finances. An older son headed south to work at Cymmer and Llew followed as soon as he could.

His early ring successes impressed no less a figure than former featherweight champion Jim Driscoll, a regular visitor to the gym above the Llwyncelyn Hotel. Driscoll took his new protégé to display his talents in Cardiff. Alas, he was flattened in two rounds. Jim kept the faith, however, and was rewarded a week later when it was the new boy's turn to land the knockout blow.

Respected manager Teddy Lewis took Edwards to the National Sporting Club and he soon became a favourite. Indeed, he was never to lose before the dinner-jacketed members at their Covent Garden base.

One victory there came over French teenager Francis Charles, later to fill out and become national champion as high as light-heavy, while Llew also excelled at the atmospheric Liverpool Stadium, where his victims included Jack Matthews, the fighting barber from Hanley, father of legendary footballer Stanley.

So much travelling meant days off work and his boss told him he had to choose; the man who hated fighting calculated that decent money could be made more quickly in the ring and left the mine forever.

The worthies of the NSC decided the young Welshman should be considered as a possible contender for their Lonsdale Belt, given up by Ted 'Kid' Lewis, and organised a series of eliminators.

First up was Joe Brooks, from Aldgate, but the bout had to be postponed after Edwards, training in Porthcawl, broke a toe while running along a country lane and had to be ferried back to the gym on a milk cart. The duo finally came face to face early in 1915. Brooks had lost to Lewis on the latter's road to the title; Edwards outpointed him twice as easily, according to the anonymous witness for *Boxing*.

Next was Fred Blakeborough, from Bradford, long on the fringe of championship status. But he stepped on the scales a pound over the limit, which meant a draining visit to a Turkish bath, coupled with an exercise regime hardly suited to someone faced with 20 rounds of boxing.

Edwards, 4–1 on at the start, never stopped moving, while Blakeborough, conscious of the need to conserve energy, was a fairly static target. A right to Fred's ear dropped him at the end of the ninth and a repeat in the 11th sent the Yorkshireman back to the deck once more. He rose at eight, but was floored again, and although he staggered upright at seven, the towel came in.

The final eliminator saw Llew take on Seaman Arthur Hayes, a one-time Driscoll victim. As early as the second, the tattooed sailor was down from a left hook; a similar blow had a similar effect in the seventh and, when the exhausted Hayes was laid beneath the ropes by a body barrage in the 10th, referee Eugene Corri rescued him from his own courage.

Finally, on May 31, 1915, Edwards met veteran Owen Moran for the title, Welsh money establishing him as favourite despite the Brummie's reputation. A former world bantam boss, he had twice drawn with Abe Attell for the feather honour in a career that was to earn him a place in the Hall of Fame in Canastota. Moran, eight years older, looked in superb condition, his tan contrasting with the pale Welshman, whose drawn features suggested that any reign at nine stone would not be long.

But Llew's greater speed was evident from the first bell, with the more muscular Moran, used to the less subtle moves of the American ring, unable to land much on his elusive opponent. Llew was understandably cautious – after all, Moran had once knocked out Battling Nelson, lauded as the 'Durable Dane' – and focussed on jabbing his way into a points lead. Owen, realising he was behind, annoyed the NSC audience by pushing Edwards away and dropping to one knee, only for Llew to resist the temptation to land the punch that would inevitably have meant disqualification.

Desperation was prompting Moran to employ one or two of the less savoury tactics he picked up across the Atlantic, landing a right uppercut while holding Llew's head in position with the left and later targeting the back of the Rhondda man's neck. But matters were to turn in the Midlander's favour.

A suspiciously low left brought a roar of disapproval from the house and a replica sent Edwards to his knees in pain. Trainer George Baillieu raced around the ring to urge his charge to rise, which he managed with some difficulty, but found the strength to keep Moran at bay

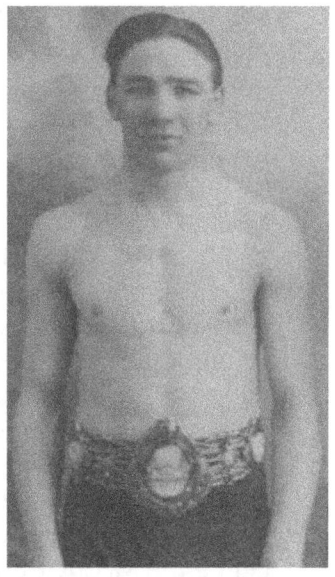

Llew shows off his Lonsdale Belt

for the rest of the round, at the end of which referee J.H. Douglas made his way to Owen's corner to deliver a belated warning.

The weakened Welshman visited the canvas twice more in the next session, Mr Douglas, seated outside the ropes, again leaving it until the interval to lecture Moran about his rough-house methods. For a minute or so of the 10th, Owen seemed chastened and attempted to box, allowing Llew to reclaim the initiative. But the Brummie seemed determined to aim for the area that had brought him dubious success and, amid a torrent of boos, landed low once too often. Mr Douglas ordered the pair apart and disqualified the offender.

The new titleholder celebrated by marrying sweetheart Margaret and turned his attention to the lucrative scene Down Under, where a huge interest in boxing was not matched by the quality of its home-grown practitioners. As a result, promoters such as 'Snowy' Baker – a 1908 Olympic boxing medallist, who also swam at those London Games, as well as playing scrum-half for Australia – were offering generous money to British boxers willing to travel.

Edwards was given a farewell dinner in Porth, where 150 admirers presented him with a gold watch. Others were less inclined to cheer a man who was leaving a country at war, while colleagues such as Driscoll and the unfortunate Percy Jones were all wearing khaki.

Nevertheless, Llew made an immediate impact in Australia, thrilling 6,000 fight-starved fans at the Sydney Stadium at Rushcutters Bay – where Jack Johnson had won the world heavyweight title – on December 18, 1915, and acquiring the Empire title, dormant since Driscoll claimed it seven years earlier.

National champion Jimmy Hill, having been down no fewer than eight times, retired after the 13th round. Hill's cornerman, Tommy Uren, tried to keep his man going, reminding him that it was for the championship of the British Empire.

Hill was unmoved. "Blast the Empire," he responded. "Edwards can have all of it!"

But Llew had again needed the steam room to make the weight and it was no surprise when he relinquished both his belts to move up a division. Aussie lightweight boss Herb McCoy was widely outpointed in Sydney, before getting the benefit of a little hometown judging in two draws in Melbourne. Llew was happy to risk a repeat when McCoy finally put his crown on the line on November 11, 1916, and this time the referee saw things the same way as other observers, giving the Welshman the championship of his new country.

A rematch in Sydney on March 10, 1917, underlined Edwards's supremacy, with Herb counted out in the 18th, and there were two further knockouts before the McCoy camp were entirely convinced.

There was one man with whom Llew had a lot more trouble. Harry Stone, a Jewish New Yorker known to enter the ring smoking a large cigar, had

Llew (second left) with George Baillieu and touring Aussies in 1920

two wins and a draw over Edwards, but when the pair met for the title of their adopted homeland in Brisbane in late 1917, Llew did enough to take the verdict.

By 1919 those around Llew raised their sights. Baillieu was sent to the US to offer Benny Leonard £3,000 to defend the world title against him in Sydney, but Freddie Welsh's conqueror could not be persuaded. Instead Edwards and his mentor settled for a trip to the Philippines, where the sport was growing in popularity. Among those Llew advised was Pancho Villa, later to end Wilde's career.

When he returned to Australia, Edwards realised he was on the slide. Money was now the main attraction and he headed for the US and a guaranteed $5,000 to face Milwaukee's Ritchie Mitchell in his home city. A glancing blow in the first round closed the Welshman's left eye and Baillieu threw in the towel after six rounds.

Promoter Tommy Andrews gave Edwards the green light to travel to Britain while his eye healed. When he arrived, he was promptly named to challenge Bermondsey's Bob Marriott, the newly crowned British lightweight boss, a decision which did not go down well with the other contenders, including

Harry Stone, the transplanted Yank who ended Llew's career

Rhondda boy Billy Fry. There was also still much anger over his decision to leave during wartime, and it was little surprise that after one fight – a three-round win in Sheffield – Llew headed back to the States, where any hope of challenging Leonard vanished with a second-round hammering by Canadian Clonie Tait.

He set sail for Australia, but his eyes were beginning to fail him and there were also problems with a damaged nerve in one leg. His old tormentor, Stone, had claimed the belt while Llew was travelling, and successfully defended against the Welshman, cutting him badly on the way to a points verdict in Melbourne on April 23, 1921.

And it was 'Hop Harry' who brought down the curtain on Llew's career when they met for the sixth time some 10 months later. By this stage he could hardly see across the ring and was taking a hiding when Baillieu pulled him out before the halfway mark. The faithful George made it clear that there should be no more and Edwards followed his advice.

He did not leave the scene entirely, travelling the outback with 'Snowy' Flynn's booth and occasionally flirting with the idea of a comeback. He also set up a school to pass on his ring knowledge; one of his pupils even called himself Young Llew Edwards and was good enough to win a national belt.

More mundanely, he earned a crust repairing boilers, while living with new partner Ethel in the Melbourne suburb of Carlton. He died in Brisbane, aged 72, but his ashes were interred with those of Ethel in Melbourne six years later.

RHYS EDWARDS
(2000-)

● Commonwealth Youth Bronze Medallist 2017

The coronavirus pandemic came at just the wrong time for the youngster from Penygraig. The foundations had been laid, the experience garnered from facing a series of ringwise journeymen was in the memory bank. And then, as Rhys Edwards looked forward to stepping up and chasing titles, everything stopped.

While boxers across the board suffered from the initial shutdown in the sport, the major promoters gradually revived their businesses with half-size bills behind closed doors, sustained by television money. For the likes of Edwards, beyond the camera's reach, there was nothing.

When the nine-year-old walked the short distance from home to the Rhondda ABC gym in the same street, coach Ivor Bartlett told him he needed to be a year older to join. But as soon as he learned that the boy's father was popular local fight nut Mansel, 'Pete' – as he is known to all – ushered him inside. The ring became his second home.

His efforts were soon rewarded with trophies. OK, he was beaten in his first Welsh schools final by Rhondda rival Jordan Withers, but he won the next two. The rivalry with Withers continued at junior level, Rhys seeing off the Ystrad redhead to win one year, but losing the following season as Jordan claimed the crown. With Withers moving up in weight, there was nobody to prevent Edwards enjoying two successes as a youth and each time he went on to claim gold at the GB championships as well.

When he ventured further afield to European and world tournaments he was unlucky with the draw, twice clashing with the eventual champion in his opening bout. But the 2017 Commonwealth youth

Rhys Edwards

event in the Bahamas finally found the valley boy on the podium, despite being among the youngest in his class.

First up in Nassau was Ulsterman Dominic Bradley, a Derry lad who had won the all-Ireland title; Rhys outboxed him for a 4-1 decision. The quarter-final saw him in with Canadian southpaw Thomas Chabot, who proved a tougher nut to crack. Two judges, in fact, voted for the Quebecois, but the other three agreed that Edwards should go through to the last four.

There the Rhondda teenager faced Charles Frankham, the grandson of former British light-heavy king Gipsy Johnny Frankham and a medallist at European and world level. The Englishman, eight months older, proved too much, taking a 5-0 verdict on his way to gold.

Edwards continued to spend four days a week training with the Wales squad in Cardiff, but without any opportunities to put what he was learning into effect. He decided it was time to go pro and signed with London-based promoter Mo Prior, Gary Lockett coming on board as his trainer.

The new adventure began with two outings at the iconic York Hall in Bethnal Green, His debut was against a fellow-Welshman in Caerphilly's Robbie Forster, who was comfortably outpointed before Rhys showed his power to halt Swindon trier Joe Beeden in two.

With manager Prior now putting on regular shows in Wales, Edwards appeared in Newport and Cardiff as well as his trips to the East End. He also began to face imported opposition, with four consecutive bouts against Spanish-based Nicaraguans, bookended by a trio of East Europeans. Three of the imports were stopped; the other four went the distance, but lost every round.

The first man to win a session against the dominant youngster was Jonny Phillips, from Sandhurst, who – perhaps not coincidentally – was Rhys's first rival with more victories than defeats on his resumé. Edwards still emerged with a 59-55 decision.

A month later life was in lockdown. Ironically, Phillips has fought twice since, dutifully losing each time to unbeaten Matchroom prospects. The Welshman, on the other hand, has gone more than a year without action because his promoter lacks TV backing. A series of day jobs were needed to pay the bills, factory work and a stint as a roofer leading to employment as a hotel waiter when Covid restrictions began to ease.

But boxing remains his driving force. The talent is still there, as is the enthusiasm. The opportunities will surely follow as the world returns to normality.

RALPH EVANS
(1953–)

🥊 Olympic Bronze Medallist 1972

Joe Bugner was a Marmite sort of fighter as far as British fans were concerned. Some loved him, more loathed him. But he played a major part in helping a Rhondda teenager win an Olympic medal.

Ralph Evans was a latecomer to boxing, despite the fact that father Gwyn had been an NCB champion. Having spent his early years in the now demolished 1, Rosehill Terrace, Gilfach Goch, he entered his teens in Waterlooville, a small town on the outskirts of Portsmouth, where he preferred racing pigeons.

Unlike Mike Tyson, it didn't take the slaughter of one of his favourite birds to prompt him to learn to fight. It was seeing kid brother Wayne bringing home trophies and getting his picture in the local paper. When Gwyn set up a new amateur club, Ralph was in.

His southpaw talent was immediately obvious. He packed in 27 bouts in his first year, racing to the British Schools final and celebrating when a body shot left his opponent unable to beat the count. Unfortunately, his joy was premature: the referee thought the blow low and disqualified young Evans.

When he reached the National Association of Boys' Clubs final the following season, he lost a split decision to future pro star Pat Cowdell. The winners were to receive Joe Bugner scholarships, allowing them to train with the future heavyweight champion in Norway. Because Ralph's bout was so close, he was chosen too.

Bugner took a shine to the youngster, who became a regular visitor to his gym, staying with Joe's mother. Ralph repaid his generosity with continued success in the ring.

Having become the first Welsh ABA champion in the newly introduced light-fly division, he reached the

Ralph Evans in his Olympic blazer

British final, only to lose to Londoner Mickey Abrams. But he was picked to represent Wales at the 1971 Europeans in Madrid, losing a 3–2 vote to Italian Franco Udella despite flooring him five times. Outraged fans ripped up seats and hurled cushions into the ring, delaying the competition for several hours. And Udella went on to become a WBC champion.

Evans won gold for Wales at a multi-nations in the Netherlands and was matched with old rival Abrams in a box-off for an Olympic place. At Caerphilly's Club Double Diamond, Ralph won on points, only for the authorities, who had pencilled in Abrams as the team captain, to order a rematch. This time Mickey was stopped because of a cut eye and the selectors had to grit their teeth and pick the Welshman.

Kept waiting in the Munich ring by fellow 18-year-old Salvador García, Ralph was sufficiently relaxed to step down and sit with ringside spectators until his Mexican opponent turned up. Despite facing a fellow-southpaw for the first time as a senior, he withstood a strong finish to take a 4–1 judges' vote.

Evans then boxed brilliantly to whitewash Chilean Héctor Velásquez, making him miss wildly, and claimed another 5–0 verdict in the quarter-final against switch-hitting Ethiopian beanpole Haile Chanyalew, decking him in the first. But waiting for him in the last four was something of a legend in amateur boxing: György Gedó, a 23-year-old welder from Hungary.

Gedó had already won two golds at European level and duly dominated Ralph, leaving him bleeding from the mouth, before outclassing a North Korean in the final. In all, he competed in four Olympics.

For Ralph, however, it was almost over. He boxed just once more – and that only to help out his father after the main attraction on a club show had fallen through – announcing his retirement less than two months past his 19th birthday.

He turned to training, looking after brother Wayne in the pro sphere and succeeding his father as chief coach at Waterlooville ABC, a role he retained until stepping down to concentrate on business interests.

WAYNE EVANS
(1955–)

- British Bantamweight Challenger 1978

The defeated challenger flinched as the bandages were removed from his right hand. The knuckles were so swollen as to merge into one purple ridge of pain. But the physical agony of his damaged mitt was easier to take than the knowledge that his one and only chance of title glory had been taken from him.

When Wayne Evans took on Merthyr's British bantam king, Johnny Owen, at Ebbw Vale Leisure Centre on April 6, 1978, both were unbeaten. But not only was the Rhondda boy facing an exceptional talent with an inexhaustible supply of stamina, he was battling a significant handicap. Even his victories usually ended with a broken and bruised hand; if the damage recurred against the 'Matchstick Man', it would compound an already difficult task.

Two years earlier Evans, whose family left Gilfach Goch for the Hampshire town of Waterlooville when he was six, had outscored Ulster southpaw Paddy Graham in a final eliminator, but those fragile fingers had ruled out a tilt at another Belfast Paddy, surname Maguire, who wore the Lonsdale Belt at that time. As he waited for his injuries to heal, Wayne had to watch fellow-Welshman Owen take his place and dethrone the Irish veteran.

After a couple of rust-removing outings, he was finally battling for the throne before a packed house. And then, just a minute or so into the action, his right hand gave way again. It needed tremendous courage merely to carry on, still desperately throwing his crippled fist in a bid to keep the relentless Owen at bay.

Wayne Evans

The Evans boys: Ralph, Gwyn Jr and Wayne

His distinctive lean-back stance confused Johnny for a while, but it merely delayed the inevitable. The taller Owen used his longer reach to land solidly and was totally in command by the middle rounds. The ninth brought the first knockdown and Wayne waved his injured hand in despair as he returned to the stool. Yet still he emerged for the next.

It was a last hurrah. Owen stormed in, Evans sagged against the ropes, his arms by his sides, and referee Jim Brimmell stepped between them. Wayne slid to the canvas and sat there for a full minute before rising to acknowledge his conqueror.

Having seen his middle son show early promise in the ring, father Gwyn founded Waterlooville ABC, whose colours Wayne wore to a clutch of junior honours before reaching the senior ABA final, only to lose a majority verdict to Stewart Ogilvie. He had proudly worn a Welsh vest, but, as he had not qualified via their area, the Welsh ABA took umbrage. The resultant row prompted him to turn pro.

His father took out a licence to manage him, with big brother Ralph looking after the training side. A string of successes was capped by a first-round demolition of British fly champion John McCluskey – the Scot was actually five pounds heavier than his novice foe and never boxed again – to establish himself as one to watch.

But a workman is only as good as his tools and in the end Wayne's weapons let him down.

TOMMY FARR
(1913–1986)

- World Heavyweight Challenger 1937
- British and Empire Heavyweight Champion 1937–38
- Welsh Heavyweight Champion 1936–37, 1951–53
- Welsh Light-Heavyweight Champion 1933–35

If legend is to be believed, no-one in Wales went to bed on the night of August 30, 1937. The whole population was huddled around the wireless as a crackling voice described events over 3,000 miles away. One of their own was challenging the immortal Joe Louis for the world heavyweight title – and what's more he was giving the champion all the trouble he could handle.

Tommy Farr had come a long way from 3, Railway Terrace, Blaenclydach, where he was born 24 years earlier, the third youngest of eight children. Their father, George, born in Cardiff to a Herefordshire family – not from Ireland, as is usually claimed – was a hard man who relished the mountain fighting by which the gamecocks of the valleys established their pecking order. But when Tommy's mother, Sarah, died at the age of 32, he disintegrated. His broken heart was soon to be hidden in a broken body: a stroke left the once powerful miner paralysed, unable to speak, dependant on his offspring for survival.

Tommy Farr – man about town

The plaque in Blaenclydach – with wrong date

Selling clothes and herb beer door to door, they scavenged the money to maintain the family and feed their father for the five remaining years of his life. And while still at school, young Thomas George laced on the gloves in a bid to add a few pence to the kitty. He was a flyweight, still short of his 14th birthday, when he earned 3s 6d (17 1/2p) for a six-round contest at Clydach Vale. And as soon as it was legally possible to leave the classroom, he began work in the pits of Blaenclydach and Llwynypia – "It was the area: you had to go into the mines, you couldn't go out and do ballet" – collecting just 11s 9d (58 1/2p) for his week's labour.

Tommy hated the life and had visions of making a living through boxing. That he did so successfully could be credited to one man. Job Churchill had lost a leg underground and set himself up as a saddler; he also became the young Farr's new father-figure, and encouraged him in his dreams. The foundations of his fistic education came through two years in Joe Gess's boxing booth, where he took on all-comers for a few bob and his keep.

Earnings from the ring were supplemented in the summer by work in the kitchens of Devon hotels. Eventually, although he was still only 16, his Post Office account held £109, enough to buy the family home in Court Street, where he proceeded to look after his younger brother and sister in what he described as "years of sublime happiness".

Time may have gilded the memory, for in his late teens Tommy was desperate enough to walk to London in a bid to find regular work. A few weeks' back-breaking toil in the stoke-hole of a Thames rubbish barge, coupled with casual jobs, in no way compensated for his homesickness, and the wanderer returned to the Rhondda, older, wiser, but no richer.

It was clear that the Farr fists held the only hope of an end to the cycle of poverty. The purse money may have been limited, but the astute Churchill supplemented it with bets on his prodigy's ability as he saw off most local rivals. London again beckoned, and Tommy, just 20 but now a well-built 12st, ventured to the Crystal Palace to face the up-and-coming Eddie Steele. Wearing a gumshield for the first time, the Welshman never felt comfortable and a right hook knocked the ill-fitting item halfway down his throat. Choking and spluttering, he leapt in panic from the ring; a slap on the back solved the problem, but the fight had been given to Steele. Shamefaced, Tommy headed back to the valleys.

At home he was still a hero. Tonyrefail's George Smith was floored five times to earn Farr the right to meet Randy Jones, from Pontarddulais, for the Welsh light-heavy title on July 22, 1933, in Tonypandy's Empire Theatre, where the ring, set up on the stage, had a slope of at least two feet. It made little difference. Although Jones, slower, but determined, rocked the local man with a right in the last, the verdict was never in doubt. Now perhaps he would get respect in the Smoke!

Eddie Phillips, a coach driver from Bow, was floored in the first at Holborn Stadium, but recovered to edge a disputed decision. When the pair were rematched in a final eliminator for the British crown, Tommy was controversially disqualified for a low blow. He finally broke his London duck against French-Canadian Charlie Belanger at Wandsworth, and, when Len Harvey abdicated his throne, it was the Rhondda boy who faced Phillips for the vacancy before a large crowd at Mountain Ash Pavilion.

But a hand injury and weight-making difficulties combined to inhibit Farr. The Londoner's clever boxing trumped the two-fisted aggression of the Rhondda man, who was also troubled by a cut over the right eye from the fifth round. Phillips allowed Tommy to expend a lot of energy over the first half of the fight, his defensive work ensuring he emerged comparatively unscathed to step up his own workrate and dominate the closing stages.

Tommy shifted his base to the Dolphin Hotel, Slough, where £2 7s 6d (£2.37) bought him a week's board and lodging and the use of a gymnasium downstairs. He also acquired a manager: Ted Broadribb, a bricklayer's son from Walworth who, under the name Young Snowball, had stopped the teenage Carpentier in Paris a quarter of a century earlier.

Farr won there himself, decisioning Presidio Pavesi on a bill promoted by American Jeff Dickson, an important man to impress. In due course Dickson turned to Farr as an opponent for former world light-heavy king Tommy Loughran, then in London. The Philadelphia stylist may have been past his best, but he was on an unbeaten run of seven fights when the Tonypandy youngster pipped him over 10 rounds at the Albert Hall. At least, he was given the decision. At the final bell, Broadribb had jumped through the ropes and congratulated Tommy for "skating it". Legendary *Daily Mirror* sports writer Peter Wilson insisted that referee Wilfred Smith, handling his first big fight, had begun to walk towards Loughran, heard Broadribb's comment and turned back to raise Farr's hand.

Tommy collected a few bonus pounds from wagers placed by the faithful Job, and thought his win entitled him to a crack at Welsh rival Jack Petersen, by now British heavyweight champion. The Board of Control disagreed – and a few indiscreet comments on the matter left Tommy further in the cold.

Trainer Tom Evans admires the Lonsdale Belt after Tommy beat Ben Foord

Another former world light-heavy king, Bob Olin, who doubled as a New York stockbroker, went the same way as Loughran – again, many thought the visitor, who decked Farr in the ninth, was unlucky – but there was still no sign of a chance at Petersen. Tommy followed Job Churchill's advice and moved back to Wales, picking up the Welsh heavyweight crown on September 14, 1936, by knocking out Big Jim Wilde – who had previously held him to a draw – with body shots at the Vetch Field in his native Swansea. The Board had recognised the bout as a final eliminator for the British crown, but, with Petersen still finding his challengers elsewhere, Tommy kept active with a points win over French champion Charles Rutz. It paid him just £50.

Yet within nine months he would be fighting for a purse 20 times the size; 1937 was Farr's annus mirabilis. It started as a spectator at Harringay, where Tommy saw Walter Neusel power to his third win over the elusive Petersen, who had already lost his title to South African-born Ben Foord. The heavyweight scene was now wide open.

Soon came the inevitable offer, from Sydney Hulls, the former Wembley promoter now heading the team at Harringay. Would Tommy top the bill on March 15 in a title fight with Foord?

As a spectacle, the bout was colourless in the extreme. Farr, despite his shorter reach, outjabbed the champion, refusing to join in a slugging match. Tommy, who had shed a stone and a half during his preparation, needed his excellent conditioning to withstand Ben's late rally, but finished a clear winner. Among the underwhelmed onlookers was a former world heavyweight champion: Max Baer.

Boxing's 'Clown Prince' had agreed to visit London and fight for Hulls, but intended opponent Petersen was now ruled out, eye trouble having forced his retirement. Farr, however uninspiringly, had removed Foord from the frame, and the Board vetoed the suggestion that Neusel should step in; two foreigners could not meet each other in a British ring. With Max already the talk of London, Hulls had to cash in on the publicity. Tommy was the only feasible foe.

If the Foord clash had been disappointing, there was no such criticism of the battle with Baer. The Harringay crowd were enthralled as Tommy, irritated by the American's ornate dressing-gown and wisecracking manner, went after him from the opening bell. Max never found an answer to Farr's left lead, allied to speed and movement. He launched a desperate assault in the last two rounds, Tommy happy to engage in toe-to-toe action, but there was little doubt about referee C.H. Douglas's verdict.

The triumph was celebrated with fish and chips and a game of cards back at Tommy's training quarters at Blackheath. There was to be no flash living while Job Churchill was around. Even the hero's pleas to spend some of his new-found wealth on a new suit and a small car were quickly silenced.

Among those surprised by Farr's victory was top sports writer Trevor Wignall, originally from Swansea. Outraged fans in Tonypandy are said to have burned his effigy in their disgust.

Next came Neusel, the man who had ended Petersen's career. The London sceptics again had Farr a wide outsider, but the Welshman was sure the German was made for him. The sight of the Nazi ambassador, von Ribbentrop, laughing and joking at ringside added to Tommy's determination. The pre-fight announcements – in Welsh, English and German – seemed endless, but the delay merely gave Tommy the chance to urge Job to get an extra £100 laid that he would win inside the distance. His insistence on standing toe to toe with Neusel worried his handlers, who had seen Petersen founder because of the same bravado, but Farr himself was in no doubt.

"I was measuring him like a tailor," he recalled. "I wanted him to be perfect for me when I was ready to go."

After two rounds Neusel's confidence was already beginning to crumble and the Welshman knew the time had come. He feinted to draw the German in before bringing over a thunderous left, which rocked him. Two follow-up rights sent Neusel crashing, one arm stretched along the bottom rope. Walter was sitting up by the time the count reached four, but he was unable to rise any further. As the count was completed, von Ribbentrop stalked coldly from the hall.

The winner's bank balance, swelled by astutely negotiated purses and even more shrewdly placed bets, was now sufficiently healthy for the careful Churchill to agree to the purchase of a car. And more was on the way, with Farr guaranteed £7,000

Tommy (facing) upsets Max Baer

to meet Neusel's compatriot, Max Schmeling, in London. But the transatlantic phone line was buzzing: Schmeling was looking for a crack at the new champion, his former victim, Joe Louis, and had no intention of risking it by facing Tommy. The truth was revealed when Sol Strauss, the cigar-chewing aide of fight czar 'Uncle Mike' Jacobs, turned up at a lunch at Eastbourne, where Farr and his new motor had won a concours d'élégance. Strauss told the amazed Welshman that Schmeling had indeed been in touch with Jacobs, but was asking too high a price. Instead, it was he, Farr, who was wanted as the first challenger for the 'Brown Bomber'.

Jacobs laid on luxurious training facilities at the Long Island resort of Long Branch, where the mayor, Alton Evans – himself of Welsh descent – gave him the freedom of the city. Some callers at the camp, like Jack Dempsey, were impressed by the visitor; others less so, notably the English writer who expressed the view that Tommy had as much chance of beating Louis as Shirley Temple.

The champion himself did not know how to take Farr. As they posed for pre-fight pictures, Joe spotted the scars on Tommy's back, the legacy of his days in the pit. He inquired as to their cause. "I used to wrestle with tigers in a circus," came the straightfaced reply.

Not everyone at home was giving Farr their full support. The British Board issued a statement days before the fight, indicating that they considered it no more than an eliminator, with the winner to face Schmeling for the title. The Americans laughed and carried on with business. Had Tommy won, he would have been recognised as world heavyweight champion by everyone except his national authority. The National Sporting Club, pointedly, paid for an £800 gold belt to be presented to the winner.

Bad weather meant a four-day postponement, a delay which enabled Farr to shed a few superfluous pounds. He still tipped the scales at 14st 8 1/2lb, half a stone heavier than the American. The pair – Farr's silk dressing gown decorated with the Welsh dragon which had adorned Freddie Welsh's shorts when he won the world lightweight crown 23 years earlier – finally squared up before 40,000 enthusiastic fans at New York's Yankee Stadium, where the promoters had allocated a special enclosure for the Welsh fans "so that they could join in song". It was marked by a Welsh flag, donated to Farr by the *Western Mail*. Meanwhile around 5,000 crammed into the Assembly Halls back in Tonypandy to listen to the radio commentary by Canadian Bob Bowman. Neither group was to be disappointed.

Farr was wary at first, giving ground as he studied the champion, and it allowed Louis to take the early rounds. Only in the third did Tommy move forward, scoring at close range, but the exchange ended with the Welshman cut beneath both eyes. Joe's straight left was proving a problem, although Tommy's elusiveness prevented the holder from getting in his dangerous right.

The Empire in Tonypandy was packed to listen to the Louis fight

When Louis finally landed the punch cleanly, in the fifth, there was a gasp from the crowd as they realised Farr had taken it in his stride, coming back to share the round.

"Louis didn't expend one scrap of energy," said Tommy later. "He shuffled to you and he was stealthily creeping up on you all the time. He was dynamite. When he hit you it was like being in the middle of an explosion."

In the sixth two solid lefts jolted Joe backwards and a right caught him as he came off the ropes; only the bell interrupted the lesson, and the Welshman was smiling as he returned to his stool. Louis stepped up the pace in the seventh, his left jab landing repeatedly, before trapping Tommy in a corner and pummelling him mercilessly. Yet somehow Farr recovered well enough to edge the eighth and ninth, only for the 10th to bring blood streaming down his battered features as Joe regained control. By the 12th, however, the champion's own right eye was bleeding and, encouraged, Tommy stormed back into the attack.

But despite the challenger's desperate attempt to land a single decisive punch, Louis was scoring regularly with the straight left and the game

Tommy lands a left jab on Louis

Welshman was forced on to the retreat. The final round saw Farr out for work early before launching an all-out assault, matching the 'Brown Bomber' punch for punch and driving him across the ring. But the bell came too soon for Tommy. Louis was still standing – and still champion.

There were boos mixed with the cheers when the verdict was announced, but Farr had no complaints: "I thought Louis just about shaded it. He shaded me with those early left jabs, and I had the forehead to prove it. It makes my nose bleed just to think about him."

The gallant defeat saw Tommy's popularity reach new heights and in a bid to cash in, he released a record, *Remember Me*, accompanied by George Formby on the ukulele, with his own composition, *Maybe I'll Find Somebody Else*, on the other side. One Fleet Street critic harshly wrote, "As a singer, Farr is a good boxer."

When he returned to the US just before Christmas, against the advice of old retainer Churchill, there were question marks over the Welshman's commitment. Following his heroics against Louis, he was introduced to Hollywood society by actor and former fighter Victor McLaglen and spent more time partying with socialite Eileen Wenzell than he did in the gym. Whether or not fitness was an issue, former champion James Braddock, old rival Baer, Californian Lou Nova and Jack Dempsey's protégé, Clarence 'Red' Burman, all claimed points victories; only in the case of Baer did Farr admit the justice of the result.

He was equally unhappy with events at home, where the Board were insisting that he defend his domestic titles against his old nemesis, Eddie Phillips. Farr relinquished the belts amid an angry tirade in the *News of the World*, which resulted in a High Court hearing and a public apology.

Back in the fold, Tommy gained revenge over Burman at Harringay, before halting former Commonwealth champion Larry Gains in front of almost 40,000 at Ninian Park and visiting Dublin to knock out Manuel Abrew. Then World War II intervened.

Farr immediately joined the RAF, despite concern over his eyesight, but he was discharged after his health broke down and he needed surgery for ear and breathing problems, a lung infection then meaning further time in a nursing home. He had to settle for touring the camps, entertaining those that military doctors deemed fitter than him. A return to the ring seemed unlikely.

There were also changes in his personal life, with the arrival of Muriel Montgomery Germon, a red-haired beauty always known as 'Monty'; and, once his health was restored, the pair settled in Brighton, where they had three children. The youngest, Gary, enjoyed his own fame in the 1960s with his band, the T-Bones.

Tommy invested in several properties in Sussex, including a restaurant and a pub, the Royal Standard, though he lost the licence after being convicted for assault following an incident in which he evicted a group of troublesome naval cadets. He also had an interest in a bookmaker's business, but it was no more successful than his attempt to enter politics: he stood for the local council in 1942, as an independent, but polled only four votes.

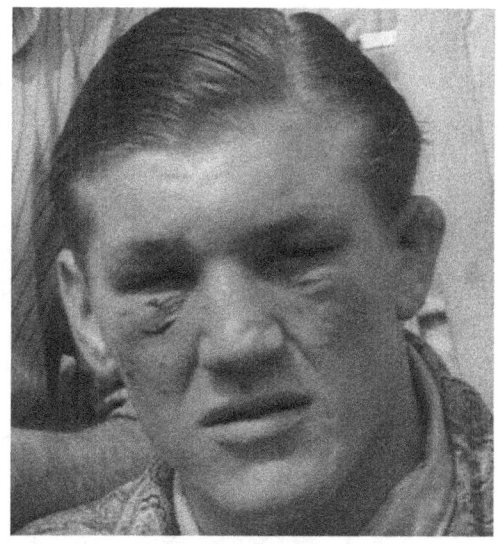

Tommy shows the scars of his gallant effort against Louis

Eventually, Farr's financial problems were such that he was forced to lace on the gloves once more. By most standards, his comeback was successful, despite an early setback after the Board, who wished to judge his suitability for a British title bid, asked that he face a domestic foe instead of repeated imports. Rhondda promoter Albert Davies hired a converted bus garage in Porth and matched Tommy with an unsung puncher from Yorkshire, Frank Bell. The grocer from Barnoldswick may have been limited, but he had power in his right hand and, when he landed cleanly in the second round, it floored the veteran. As Farr rose, Bell repeated the dose, sending him face-first to the canvas. The stunned silence was broken only by the referee's count and the heavy breathing of the local hero, knocked out for the only time in his career.

But it was not the end. Soon Farr was reclaiming his old Welsh heavyweight crown by dethroning Dennis Powell on July 7, 1951, a bout which actually took place in England at the West Midlands Showground in Shrewsbury.

Powell, born in Monmouthshire, but long resident in the Mid-Wales village of Four Crosses, had been allowed to listen to the Louis fight as a 12-year-old hospital patient and Farr was his idol. Really a light-heavy, at which weight he later won a Lonsdale Belt, he conceded 20lb to his hero, but, at 26, the

Tommy chats with mentor Job Churchill on a trip back home in 1939

calendar was on his side. His aggressive opening had Farr focussing on defence, but things changed when a clash of heads in the fifth reopened an old wound above Dennis's left eyebrow. Tommy did what he had to do, his accurate punches worsening the injury to the extent that referee Ike Powell called a halt at the end of the following episode.

It was another youthful rival who ended Farr's second coming. On March 9, 1953, Tommy took on Don Cockell at Nottingham Ice Stadium in a fight that would earn the winner a shot at the British title, then held by North Walian Johnny Williams. Farr, just three days before his 40th birthday – though he claimed, throughout his life, to be a year younger – nevertheless began as favourite against the former blacksmith from Battersea, whose fleshy appearance meant he was rarely given his due as a boxer.

Cockell's spare tyre certainly did not hamper him on this occasion. He kept his jab in Tommy's face, cutting his ageing skin in several places, although a combination of the Welshman's defensive nous and Don's lack of power meant there were no knockdowns. But at the end of seven one-sided rounds, referee Eugene Henderson walked to the Farr corner and signalled the end of a great career. Tommy, after a brief protest, took the microphone and led the Welsh members of the 6,000 crowd in *Hen Wlad fy Nhadau*. It was a tuneful swansong.

The comeback had achieved its principal purpose: the taxman was paid, most debts were settled – there were still a few embarrassing court cases to get through – and his children's education was secured. With the ring behind him for good, he earned a few quid as a columnist with the *Sunday Pictorial* and then worked for a firm which sold industrial paint. He died from cancer, aged 72, at home in Shoreham on St David's Day, 1986.

Tommy Farr won many more than he lost, but owes his immortality to his gallantry in defeat that August night in New York. As he put it himself, "For one glorious hour of triumph but not of victory, fame lifted me upon the shoulders of men." He sits there still.

BILLY FRY
(1895–1958)

- Welsh Featherweight Champion 1918–21
- Welsh Welterweight Champion 1930–31

It would be a gross slander to suggest that most boxers' reading habits rarely extend beyond the racing pages. But surely few can have agreed to a short-notice fight because of a love of Charles Dickens. Billy Fry did.

When the call came for a 24-hour substitute to tackle one-time British bantam king Tommy Noble in London, the Rhondda man leapt at the chance. He had been reading *The Old Curiosity Shop* and was keen to visit the establishment said to have inspired the author.

On arrival at Paddington, Billy headed off to Westminster to pursue his quest, eventually turning up at the venue, boxing gear in one hand and the book in the other, an hour late for his engagement. Noble was not best pleased; he was even less happy 20 rounds later, when the Welshman's hand was raised.

William Henry Fry was born at Blaenllechau, the son of a Somerset-born collier, and, inevitably, followed his father down the pit. A couple of years later, the 16-year-old was also earning with his fists and his natural talent was obvious.

As well as the impatient Noble, Wales's own Bill Beynon was another former British champion among his victims, while on Boxing Day 1917 Fry halted Jimmy

Billy Fry

Wilde's old rival, Tancy Lee, who had just claimed the featherweight Lonsdale Belt. Their meeting, at Liverpool Stadium, was made at 9st 2lb, so the title was not at stake, and Billy was said to look substantially heavier than that. He "had neglected to get into thorough condition", claimed *Boxing*'s reporter, but he still proved too fast for the Scot, who shipped regular punishment before finally succumbing to a right uppercut in the 19th.

The comment about Fry's fitness was not uncommon. A rare visitor to the gym, he was said to train on fish and chips and his appearance for one fight was likened to "a second-hand barrel". He could get down to featherweight with a little effort, however, and managed it when he contested the vacant Welsh championship at the National Sporting Club on March 4, 1918.

In the opposite corner was Danny Morgan, from the Tirphil clan, who had outpointed Billy four months earlier and also claimed a victory over Lee. Those who saw a forgettable encounter can be forgiven for wondering how Tancy managed to lose to either. But once Fry had overcome an early tendency to slap, he was in total control and took an undisputed decision.

It earned him a chance at Lee's British crown, but the battle with the scales proved too much. Sparring with Treherbert's Jim Culverhouse in a sweltering Wattstown gym, Billy fainted and was pulled out of the championship challenge; Morgan replaced him, but lost on points.

Both Welshmen moved up to lightweight, with a rubber match at Llwynypia Baths in February 1921 seen in some quarters as disputing the national crown. Fry gained the nod, but most recognised another Tirphil man, Arthur Evans, as the rightful champion.

Billy seemed to lose interest and was described as "very corpulent" in defeat against Newport's Jack Blackborow, eventually dropping out of sight for four years.

Returning in late 1927 with renewed enthusiasm, he racked up several victories before applying for consideration by the newly formed Welsh Association and Control Board as a contender for the Welsh light title now held by Crumlin farmer Edgar Evans. He was matched in an eliminator with London-based Haydn Williams, but lost against another hopeful, Gordon Cook, who was handed a straight shot and dethroned Evans.

An alternative view of Billy

Fry, who blamed weight-making problems for the reverse, headed for the welterweights.

With Newport's Ben Marshall touring Australia, Billy began to call himself the "resident" champion and his claim had enough legitimacy for the Board to order a mandatory defence when Marshall returned. Ben rejected what he saw as an inadequate purse for the job and was promptly stripped, leaving Fry to face Danny Evans, with whom he had already drawn, for the vacant title.

Their meeting, in Pontypridd on November 10, 1930, was surprisingly one-sided. The Glanamman fighter was badly cut over the left eye in the middle rounds, but was already falling behind, as the veteran Fry dominated without ever producing anything spectacular.

Things were very different in the rematch 10 months later on Danny's territory at the Pavilion in Ammanford. The challenger built an early lead despite Fry's clever defence and although a rusty Billy finally found his rhythm to enjoy a good seventh, Evans regained control and battered the champion for the next few sessions. Fry dug deep to stage a strong finish, but Evans was the fitter, stepping up the pace to walk through Billy's jab and hand out some solid punishment.

Billy was just 10 days short of his 36th birthday and soon opted to hang up the gloves. But anyone who wins two Welsh titles a dozen years apart deserves his place in the history books – even if they aren't written by Dickens.

DARRON GRIFFITHS
(1972–)

- Welsh Super-Middleweight Champion 1993–99

- Welsh Cruiserweight Champion 1999–2000

For most people, it would be enough to boast that you won national crowns at two different weights. But for the talented southpaw from Porth, there was a sense of unfulfilled promise. After all, he took part in five British title eliminators and still never boxed for the Lonsdale Belt.

The story began at Gilfach Goch ABC, where nine-year-old Darron followed big brother Paul – later to die tragically young in a motorcycle accident – and learned the basics from coach Ken McCann, picking up the first two of his four Welsh schoolboy titles. A switch to the Rhondda club's base at Penygraig saw father Dai, along with Pete Bartlett, guide him to further junior honours and a Welsh senior championship in 1990, when Scot Steve Wilson outpointed him in the British final.

The pro game beckoned. Griffiths signed with former heavyweight Billy Aird, who optimistically predicted he would be Britain's best middleweight since Terry Downes. Steady progress took the Porth southpaw into contention and his first eliminator victory, over Yorkshireman Colin Manners, on a dinner show in Solihull.

Aird and trainer Pat Thomas agreed that he was now a suitable bill-topper as they began to promote at Cardiff's STAR Centre, featuring him in a further eliminator against Brummie Antonio Fernandez. It brought another win, but even Darron thought Fernandez unlucky not to get referee Mickey Vann's decision.

Only 20, the builder's apprentice was still too young to box for the title and, by the time he was eligible, making 11st 6lb had become problematic. Instead, he contested the new Welsh honour up at super-middle, once again at the STAR, with Swansea window cleaner John Kaighin in the opposite corner on March 24, 1993.

Darron Griffiths

There were no doubts this time. Darron's one-twos were constantly in Kaighin's face before a rapid combination in the sixth stopped John in his tracks. When Darron resumed the attack, he kept punching until Maesteg referee Mike Heatherwick, handling his first title bout, waved it off.

Aird, disappointed by small crowds, abandoned the STAR and Darron sought pastures new, linking up with Frank Maloney, who kept him busy with four fights in four months, culminating in yet another British title eliminator, this time at 12st. Another lefty, Stepney's awkward Ray Webb, had home advantage at the York Hall – but it made no difference as Griffiths recovered from a torrid fifth to floor the Londoner twice and end matters within 48 seconds of the bell to start the sixth.

The Welshman was back in Bethnal Green five months later, favoured to win a final eliminator against Southern Area champion Ali Forbes, his longer reach helping him build a clear lead. But the 33-year-old Sydenham man took over in the middle sessions and it was nip-and-tuck until the close. Many ringsiders considered Griffiths had done enough, but referee Dave Parris disagreed.

Things went from bad to worse for Darron, with a shocking first-round defeat to fast-rising Dean Francis, even if an angry Maloney insisted that the final punch had been after the bell.

It was back to domestic duties and a defence of the Welsh belt against Cardiffian Wayne Ellis in the neutral, if exotic setting of Swansea's Brangwyn

Hall, hosting boxing for the first time. Ellis, a former middleweight ruler, who looked a little fleshy in the heavier division, was so neatly turned in the second that he was left with his head between the ropes as if examining Sir Frank Brangwyn's colourful murals. The challenger recovered to shade the middle rounds, but Griffiths, now once again under the tutelage of Pat Thomas, was generally in charge and Wayne, with blood pouring from a series of cuts, was a clear second at the end.

Unbeaten Mark Delaney retained his WBO Inter-Continental belt with a unanimous verdict in the East End and then, across the river at the Elephant and Castle, Canadian Chris Johnson, also boasting a 100 per cent record, broke the Welshman's nose and forced his corner to retire him after three painful rounds.

By now Darron was travelling in search of the cash. Defeats in Denmark and Germany were followed by a points loss to Mark Delaney's big brother, Garry, before the Porth boxer, now earning a crust as a drayman, claimed his second Welsh title at the Welsh Institute of Sport on February 23, 1999.

It came up at cruiserweight, where Dolgellau brawler Tim Redman caused a few problems with his errant head before Griffiths battered him to the canvas in the seventh. The exhausted North Walian sat out the count before walking wearily back to his corner.

An impressive stoppage of unbeaten Dubliner Cathal O'Grady was followed by a commendable draw with Turkish-born Turan Bagci in Paris and a points loss to future WBO challenger Rudiger May in Germany, earning Darron his final British title eliminator. It came at Dagenham against former WBU ruler Rob Norton and when the Dudley man's arm was lifted at the finish the gesture also marked the end of Griffiths's career.

Father-of-two Griffiths has been employed for many years in the brewing industry, but still keeps in touch with the fight scene, occasionally helping out with the kids at Gilfach Goch, where it all began.

EDDIE JOHN
(1907–1992)

🥊 Welsh Flyweight Champion 1926–29

It's tricky for the parents of boxers when two of their sons excel in the same weight division. And, like the heavyweight Klitschkos in recent times, any ideas the John boys might have had about repeating their brotherly battles for real were swiftly vetoed by mam and dad.

Edward James Northey John, the eldest boy and therefore named after his haulier father – the Northey was his mother's maiden name – had to give up the Welsh flyweight title once young Phineas emerged as a leading contender. Not that Sarah Jane was always opposed to her offspring swapping punches.

While still at school, her lads organised boxing matches in their back yard in Gelli, charging their pals a pin to come and watch – a safety pin let the donor bring a friend. Once she realised it was possible to make a profit out of pugilism, she was all for it.

Certainly Eddie wasted no time in earning a crust with his fists. He faced Idris Brace when both were 12 and by his 15th birthday he was challenging any lad in Wales at five and a half stone, boosted by the training he was receiving from Fred Higgins at the Pengelli Hotel in Cwmparc. Another Higgins pupil was younger brother Tommy.

Steady progress saw John matched with Cardiffian Frank Kestrell for the vacant Welsh flyweight crown, the pair meeting at the capital's Engineers' Drill Hall on February 14, 1927, the main attraction of a benefit night for top trainer Fred Yeates.

Kestrell gave away height and reach, but still managed to get in and out with a good left lead. But he relied too much on that single strategy, while Eddie had greater variety. Frank was soon bleeding from a reopened cut first sustained in sparring, but did well in the ninth and tenth

Eddie John

Eddie (left) and brother Phineas could never face off for real

before fading. John came on strongly to take the decision in a good scrap, worthy of the belt.

The new monarch was not too interested in defending, having moved to live in Hendon and seek fistic employment in the London rings. And later in 1927 he boarded the P & O steamship *Baradine*, along with Port Talbot's Billy Nicholas, Ystrad's Billy Evans and the returning Jack Jones, from Merthyr, to be trained in Australia by Cardiff emigrant 'Slam' Sullivan.

For John, it was a singularly unsuccessful venture. He was knocked out by Aussie bantam champ Billy McAllister – Eddie was described as "hopelessly outclassed" – and did little better in his other contents before heading back home.

With brother Phineas now chasing his fly title, Eddie applied for consideration by the newly formed Welsh Association and Control Board as a contender for the Welsh bantam throne, unoccupied following the death of Tosh Powell. But, despite a bye in the first batch of eliminators, he lost a points decision to Cardiff-based Irishman Minty Rose and returned to flyweight.

Even without the complication of fraternal involvement, Eddie may well have realised that his grasp of the title was becoming increasingly tenuous when he was floored twice and halted in 10 rounds by Merthyr's Cuthbert Taylor, having only his third paid contest, although hardly a novice as he had competed the previous summer in the Amsterdam Olympics.

A few weeks later John announced his retirement, relinquishing his belt in a letter to the Welsh Board which explained that priority had to go to his new job in London. He was only 21, but had never rediscovered his form after the disastrous tour Down Under.

Inevitably, for one so young, there were sporadic reappearances, but two years later he unlaced his gloves for the final time. He remained in England and died in Rugby, aged 85.

PHINEAS JOHN
(1910–1985)

- Welsh Flyweight Champion 1928–29

Most would have considered a name like Phineas Gladney John distinctive enough to be going on with. But when Ted Broadribb took over his management, he thought a new label was needed. So he began to promote his new charge as 'Smiling Moon'.

It was an appropriate description of the beaming, round-faced youngster from Gelli. Contemporary reports referred to his "battle-scarred dial lit up by a cheerful grin". But his achievements in the ring needed no such embellishment.

Although only three years older, big brother Eddie was already in title contention by the time Phineas turned pro in 1926. Not that it was long before the youngster was also being talked of in high places.

He outpointed Minty Rose, a Belfast boy living in Cardiff, in an official eliminator for Welsh fly honours, but the pair met again at Merthyr's Penydarren Park the following month, only for lightning and torrential rain to cause the contest to be abandoned after 12 rounds. It was rearranged for a fortnight later, when some insisted it was for the vacant title. Phineas again took the decision, but he, of all people, could hardly have been unaware that the throne was already occupied – by his brother, Eddie.

And when his two-fisted attacks proved superior to the long-distance skills of Jerry O'Neil just before Christmas 1928, Phineas found himself now the official challenger. But parental disapproval of any fraternal confrontation forced him to tell the Board that he would not accept the opportunity.

Things changed abruptly when Eddie was badly beaten by former Olympian Cuthbert Taylor and relinquished his belt. Phineas hastily recanted and, his case supported by a victory over the previously unbeaten Taylor, was matched

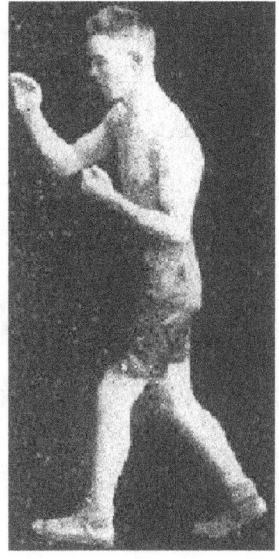

Phineas John

in a return with O'Neil for the vacant title, on March 2, 1929, in Merthyr. The Rhondda boy boxed brilliantly, and although Jerry, bleeding profusely from nose and mouth, held his own up to the 14th, John finished strongly to clinch the decision.

Setting his sights on British honours, Phineas met Manchester's Jackie Brown, whom he had already beaten, in an elimination series to find a challenger for fly boss Johnny Hill, but he was outpointed in an uninspiring contest. By the time the John met him once more in an overweight bout six months later, Brown, again a points victor, was the new champion and went on to reign for six years.

Phineas, meanwhile, was no longer ruling his own square mile. Rhondda rival Freddie Morgan dethroned him in Pontypridd on July 22, 1929, after a fight close enough for the verdict to earn Bob Hill some verbal stick from John's fans. Not only did the crowd stand and boo for several minutes, one of the loser's seconds "joined in hurling epithets of a disgraceful nature at the referee", in the words of the *Echo* reporter at ringside.

Six weeks later Phineas outboxed old foe Taylor, now the Welsh bantam boss, with an excellent display of counter-punching. Cuthbert floored Phineas in the 12th, but the Rhondda man recovered to win a toe-to-toe closing session and edge the decision. But the bout had been made at 8st 7lb and Taylor's crown was safe.

Now confirmed as a bantam, John outscored George Williams in a Welsh title eliminator, but slipped up against Terence Morgan and even a decision over Maesteg's Stan Jehu, recent conqueror of Taylor, did not earn a shot at the belt. Phineas turned his back on Wales.

Basing himself in London – and for a while in Sheffield – he fought where the money was, including a successful tour of South Africa, before emerging from 16 contestants to win a gold belt in an open featherweight competition at Manchester's Belle Vue. The prize was supposed to include a challenge to British champion Nel Tarleton, but as both were managed by Broadribb, the fight never happened.

Phineas (left) and the third boxing brother, Tommy

In 1934 Phineas and brother Tommy sailed for Sydney, but the family relationship was severely strained when Phineas was badly cut against Filipino Varias Milling. Tommy, in the corner, took one look and signalled to the referee, who declared Milling the winner. Phineas went bananas and the official retracted his decision, while the brothers had a blazing row and Tommy stormed off. By the time he returned, Phineas had won the next round, only for a doctor to examine the injury and insist

Sydney Stadium, where John suffered two cut-eye losses that caused friction in the corner and beyond

it was too severe to continue. In the end it needed the intervention of a local police inspector to convince the bloodstained warrior that the fight was over.

The wound reopened against Aussie bantam champion Merv Blandon and, although the Welshman had won every round, Tommy again retired him at the interval. This time the doctor, having checked the damage in the dressing room, disagreed and on his recommendation the promoters withheld John's purse. It took some argument before they at least agreed to pay for his passage home.

Phineas continued to campaign in top-class company until the war intervened. In 1946 the family returned to Wales, taking charge of a series of Cardiff pubs, while wife Agnes devoted herself to running football teams in the Rhondda, becoming, at the age of 78, the first woman to receive the FA of Wales long service medal. Her husband had died five years earlier.

BARRIE JONES
(1985–)

- British Welterweight Challenger 2008
- Welsh Light-Middleweight Champion 2011–14, 2015-16

For a period in the early 2010s, it seemed as though one man was single-handedly keeping the flame alive in the Rhondda. Before the emergence of Lewis Rees, Liam Williams and, more recently, Rhys Edwards, the responsibility for maintaining the valleys' fighting tradition rested on the shoulders of the Jones boy.

The stylish southpaw followed big brother Robert to Rhondda ABC at the age of nine, leaving at 16 when father Dai set up a club in their home village of Ferndale. A clutch of Welsh age-group titles suggested that his was a special talent, followed by success in his one tilt at the senior Welsh ABAs.

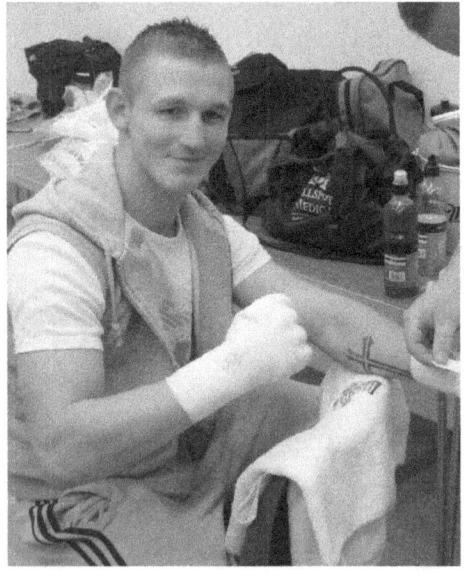

Barrie Jones prepares for battle

Top promoter Frank Warren took notice, parachuting in right-hand man Dean Powell to manage the teenager and work the corner on fight nights, while Dad still took care of the day-to-day training. The combination helped Barrie to 15 straight victories, although it must be said that only one of his victims had a winning record.

A shot at the Celtic title fell through when Scot Gary Young was injured, but Jones was paired with another Warren prospect, Tony Doherty, for the vacant Welsh welter belt. 'The Doc' had just suffered his first defeat, losing his Celtic crown somewhat controversially to future British champion Kevin McIntyre, but was still the favourite at Cardiff International Arena on March 22, 2008. And, although the target of persistent racial abuse from a couple of Barrie's less civilized supporters, the Gwent traveller took a clear decision.

Despite the setback, it was Jones who found himself in with fast-rising Kell Brook for the vacant British title three months later. Holder McIntyre was stripped after injury forced him out of a planned defence against the Yorkshireman and, with Doherty out of training, Barrie was given a short-notice opportunity.

It proved a losing gamble. Although the tall Welshman was always competitive, Brook, hitherto regarded as an under-achiever, chose this night at the York Hall to put it all together, showing uncharacteristic patience as he wore Jones down. By the sixth it had become one-sided and, 42 seconds into the seventh, with Barrie's cornerman for the night, Jimmy Tibbs, signalling surrender, referee Mickey Vann called a halt.

Jones dropped to light-welter, but suffered further blows when former WBA ruler Souleymane Mbaye was awarded a disgraceful verdict in an eight-rounder, followed by a first-stage exit from arguably the strongest-ever Prizefighter tournament.

A disastrous spell saw him halted in six rounds of a second Welsh challenge, this time at 10st, with the ringwise Jason Cook proving too strong at the Newport Centre on November 6, 2010. When unbeaten Scouser Liam Smith knocked him out in three, it seemed that Jones, now managed by Aberystwyth-based Nick Hodges, was struggling even with the role of trial horse.

But it proved third time lucky when Barrie stepped up to light-middle for another shot at the Welsh strap. Faced by combative, but limited Bargoed boy Gary Cooper at Aberdare's Sobell Centre on November 19, 2011, Jones took every round and, at last, had a professional prize.

He was due to defend against local ticket-seller Lee Churcher in Newport on May 19, 2012, but the challenger could not make 11st and the bout went ahead for the vacant middleweight crown. For eight and a half rounds, Barrie was on his way to becoming a double champion, only for one roundhouse right to scramble his senses and prompt referee Wynford Jones to call a halt.

After a year's inactivity, he relinquished the Welsh 11st title, Newport youngster Jerome Samuels emulating his father, Paul, and taking over the division. But when Jerome defended against his predecessor at the Newport Centre on March 13, 2015, Jones came out fast and regained the belt inside three rounds.

Seven months later in the same hall Barrie despatched Swansea challenger James Lilley with body shots in six, but fights falling through meant it proved his last action until he reappeared in 2018 on the bareknuckle scene, where the technical boxer has successfully reinvented himself as a puncher.

GINGER JONES
(1905–1986)

- Welsh Featherweight Champion 1929–33

Boxers are often described as being from a certain stable. In Bryn Jones's case it was literally true. The youngster learned the basics from father Will – known when he fought on the mountains as 'Billy Collier' – in a converted stable in the garden of their Ferndale home.

Ginger Jones

Becoming a professional was pretty much inevitable for someone who had seen big brother Harold contest a British title and he became a regular at Gomer Perkins's gym at the Rhondda Hotel, where Will Pearson and, later, Dai Lodwick honed his rough edges.

Ginger – his nickname needs no explanation – was a quick learner and soon found himself meeting and beating top operators like Young Allsopp and former British champion Bill Beynon. He caught the eye of Johnny Basham, a former two-weight British and European ruler, and the Newport man recommended him to Wales's top manager of the day, Johnny Vaughan, who promptly took him to live near his Ammanford base.

Jones was soon involved in an eliminating bout for the Welsh featherweight title, but his clash with Aberdare's Charlie Chew was a poor affair in sweltering heat. Referee D.W. Davies couldn't separate them, but there was no great interest in watching a repeat, and a mere week later Ginger was involved in a second eliminator, this time coming out on top when Young Freddie Welsh was disqualified. But it was more than a year before he had his shot at the championship.

With holder Charlie Stone sidelined by injury, Jones lost and won against Rhondda rival Billy Evans before the Ystrad man saw off Chew for the throne Stone was eventually forced to vacate. While awaiting his chance, Ginger became a frequent visitor to the East End's famous Premierland, on one trip outspeeding former British champion and fellow-redhead Johnny Curley.

It was on more familiar ground in Pentre that Jones took on Evans on September 21, 1929. The challenger started slowly, but began to jolt Billy with left hooks as he moved in, varying the treatment with occasional uppercuts. Although Evans staged something of a recovery in the 11th, the following session saw him repeatedly driven to the ropes and, despite a gallant rearguard action, the final bell saw the title change hands.

Ginger meets Panama Al Brown, with ref Bill Allen and promoter Teddy Lewis

Ginger crossed to Belfast and outscored 1928 Olympian Jack Garland in a British title eliminator, but the decision was noisily disputed and the Board ordered a rematch. Manager Vaughan saw no reason for this and refused, a stance that did nothing to help his man in the eyes of the authority.

Instead Jones had to settle for maintaining his dominance at home. He travelled to Wrexham's Racecourse football ground to defend against local Jim Crawford before a substantial crowd on Bank Holiday Monday, flooring his man three times early on as he won at a canter.

Old foe Evans tried to reclaim his crown at Ammanford, but some 2,000 fans watched their adopted local take a clear-cut victory, repeating the feat against Caerau's Selwyn Davies in another outing in the makeshift arena alongside the Cross Inn Hotel.

Between those defences, Ginger took on fast-rising Nel Tarleton on Merseyside in a match-up intended to put the Welshman back into British title contention. But he was floored in the fifth by a body punch and was well beaten by a top-form Nella, who went on to capture the Lonsdale Belt five months later.

But the biggest name on Jones's record was Panama Al Brown, Latin America's first world champion, who met him at Mountain Ash Pavilion on September 21, 1931. Before the bout, the capacity crowd were led in the anthem, at Brown's special request, and then, bizarrely, *Swanee River*, presumably because the visitor was black. The crowd, unguided, added *For He's a Jolly Good Fellow*.

Ginger, understandably, opened with a barrage to the midriff of the 5ft 11in Brown – taller by seven inches – and was doing well until he himself was worn down by body shots. The bout ended as the result of an uppercut to the stomach in the ninth. Jones fell to hands and knees, the fans optimistically claiming a low blow, but referee Bill Allen counted him out.

It was back to the more humdrum domestic scene, with George Fielding becoming the second Wrexham product to challenge for his belt. He even dropped Ginger in the fourth, but the holder's mobility kept him clear of further trouble until the sixth, when a right to the point of the jaw laid the North Walian on his back, unable to beat the count.

In 1933 Jones sailed for South Africa, sparring throughout the voyage, but sustaining a cut eye shortly before docking. The gash reopened when he met national champion Laurie 'Non-Stop' Stevens and after seven rounds he was forced to pull out. Despite the injury, he boxed again and won a few days later before returning home.

It was becoming increasingly difficult for Ginger to get down to nine stone and he relinquished his Welsh belt, also withdrawing from a British eliminator against Southern Area champion Tommy Rogers. But the move to lightweight brought little joy, his first outing in that division ending in a six-round stoppage by reigning British monarch Johnny Cuthbert.

With health also becoming an issue, Jones hung up his gloves and turned to the training side, while keeping active with a spot of tennis, fishing and golf. He worked in insurance, served in the Pioneer Corps during World War II and lived at Pontardawe until his death at the age of 81.

HAROLD JONES
(1900–1976)

British Bantamweight Challenger 1920

Controversy is never far away from the boxing ring. And many of the arguments that have resonated through the years have involved refereeing decisions. One such robbed Harold Jones of a Lonsdale Belt.

The Ferndale youngster was still in his teens when his opportunity came. A points victory over Salford's Jack 'Kid' Doyle in an official eliminator had earned him as shot at British bantamweight champion Walter Ross at the National Sporting Club on February 23, 1920.

However, Ross pulled out, unable to make the weight, and was replaced by fellow-Scot Jim Higgins in what was now a contest for the vacant title. All Jones knew about the replacement was that he had been Ross's sparring partner. It was hardly surprising: this was only the seventh bout of Higgins's pro career and he had lost the first three.

Jim had, however, recently knocked out Doyle and, on the basis of the pair's respective encounters with the 'Kid', the odds-makers had Higgins 2–1 on at the first bell. Perhaps the bookies underestimated Harold, who was inches taller and had a substantial reach advantage.

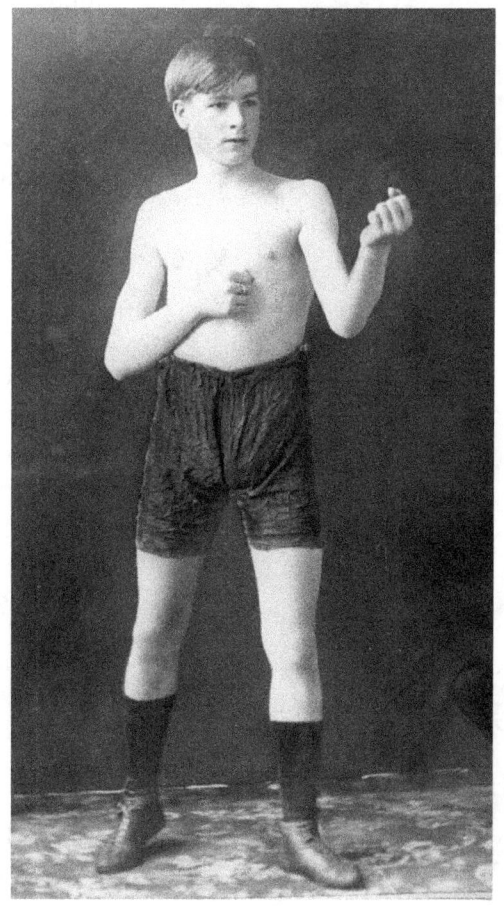

Harold Jones

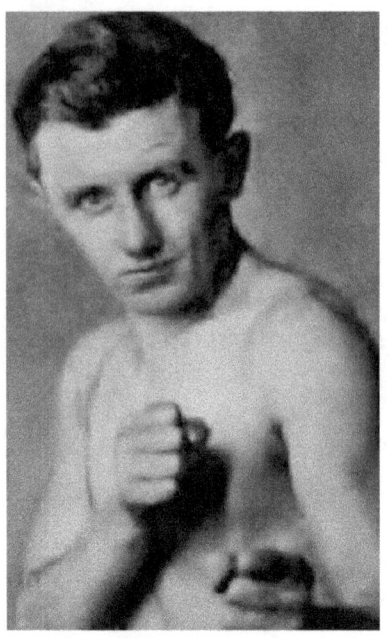

Jim Higgins, the Scot who defeated Jones for the Lonsdale Belt.

Referee J.H. Douglas

They soon changed their tune when he started strongly and then floored the Hamilton man in the seventh, the gong coming to Jim's rescue. By the tenth, Jones was 15–1 on.

But in the 13th Higgins caught the Welshman off-balance and he went down to one knee, taking a count of eight; a follow-up attack dropped him again, but once more he rose at eight, huddled on the ropes behind a crossed-arms protective shield as the Scot whaled away. Harold seemed in no great difficulty even when Higgins landed a roundhouse right to the top of the Welshman's head, but referee J.H. Douglas - father of Olympic middleweight gold medallist and England cricket captain Johnny – decided to step in and stop the contest.

The assembled members were outraged, with more than a hundred said to have penned letters of resignation in protest. There were those who thought the ending fair, however, pointing out that Jones was exhausted; others insisted that Higgins had expended a lot of energy in trying to finish matters and could himself have been vulnerable if Harold was allowed to continue.

In fact, when the bout was halted, Jones believed the bell must have gone and walked to his corner, with a steady step, expecting to resume hostilities after the interval. Even allowing for the late knockdowns, Harold seemed to be well ahead on points at the finish.

Although Jones's career lasted another 14 years, the disappointment eroded much of his early enthusiasm and, despite the unsatisfactory ending to his title shot, he was never given another.

Harold had inherited his love of fisticuffs from his father, a mountain fighter known as 'Billy Collier', with two other sons, Ginger and Henry, also useful pros. But his first blows were thrown in the unlikely surroundings of a sanatorium.

As a 15-year-old boy scout at summer camp, he was among a party taken to a house at Ystradowen in the Vale of Glamorgan, where wounded soldiers were convalescing. To entertain the troops, Jones was called up to spar with the scoutmaster and promptly bloodied the man's nose. Within months he was being paid for his punches.

Although he made good progress and was soon holding his own with some of the best around, he lost as many as he won and his leap into title contention – and at British level, not Welsh – was something of a surprise. Indeed, he was never to box for his domestic honour; when, in 1921, he was invited to take part in a tournament to arrive at a new Welsh bantam king, Harold was outpointed at the first stage by Rhondda rival Young Allsopp, and six years later he lost an eliminator to the ill-fated Tosh Powell.

He did eventually cross gloves with Ross, the man he had been intended to face for the Lonsdale Belt, but although Jones was the better boxer on the night, Walter had the strength and power and finished him in the 13th, a number that was clearly unlucky for Harold.

Jones, now living in Caerphilly, began to chase the money, criss-crossing Britain to take on some good men and, frequently, suffering for it. Future champions Bugler Harry Lake and Johnny Brown were among those who ensured the full count was tolled over the fading Welshman. Eventually Harold stepped away from the ring to focus on a new job with the railways.

There was a comeback, but this was no longer the boxer some had compared to a second Jim Driscoll, with "upright stance, fine footwork, piston-rod-like straight left, followed by straight from the shoulder rights". On his return he adopted a crouch and was almost totally defensive, focussed on spoiling tactics.

It was a disappointing, drawn-out end to a career that had once promised so much more.

JACK JONES 'SHONI ENGINEER'
(1862–1894)

- Welsh Middleweight Champion 1880s

The battling blacksmith from Treorchy was famous throughout South Wales and across the border. But not by his given name. After all, there was a Jack Jones in virtually every street. Even in the prize ring, another bearing the same handle had already achieved nationwide recognition. That Jack Jones, a farm boy from Penderyn, above Merthyr, was identified as 'Shoni Sgubor Fawr'. His Rhondda counterpart became known as 'Shoni Engineer'.

That the first 'Shoni' was transported to Australia as a convict two decades before the second was born has not prevented them being frequently confused. But the later man was equally worthy of respect for his achievements. Most of them were never recorded, having taken place as dawn broke on the bare mountains. But enough reports reached the public prints to back up the folk memories.

Shoeing the horses and pit ponies of the Rhondda helped the Jones boy build a sturdy body. And it was not long before he was putting his muscles to good use beyond the forge.

One of his earliest scraps came against Tom Davies, the son of a Pentre bookseller and therefore labelled 'Tom Books'. They met in a booth set up opposite Treherbert police station, a huge crowd including a group of chapel elders, angry that the building's occupants did not put a stop to it.

But the bout was under the recently introduced Queensberry Rules and therefore legal – until the frustrated Tom, after half a dozen brutal rounds, ripped off one glove and stuck a thumb in Shoni's eye, at which point the police stepped in. Ironically, Tom later became a deacon himself. But most of Jones's bouts were in the old style, with bare fists. He had knocked out Peter Burns, alias 'Dublin Tom', in 47 rounds, before travelling to Bristol to face a local, Jem Goytrell. Shoni, already being called "the well-known Welsh middleweight champion", was prepared in Birmingham by Bill 'Jockey' Saunders, and at 5ft 10in weighed 10st 7lb, taller and heavier than his rival.

The Welshman was on top from the start, repeatedly felling his man, but Goytrell kept coming back for more. With a session ending whenever a boxer went down, the rounds began to mount up. More than 80 had passed, each culminating in Jem's seconds dragging him to his stool, when a combination of exhaustion and the cold morning air began to tell on Shoni. Eventually, he was so weak that he was more or less pushed over by Goytrell and had no energy to answer the call.

"After 70-odd rounds my jaws kept rattling like a dice box," Jones told a *Western Mail* reporter two days later. "My legs knocked together as if I had the ague. There I was, quite unable to do anything."

Jones's dominance on home ground was rapidly being challenged by a Cardiff-Irishman, John O'Brien. The first attempt to bring them together took place outside Brecon. The Fancy had arrived in their broughams and hansom cabs, the plebs had tramped for miles across the fields, and the appointed referee, an elderly top-hatted gentleman with a battered umbrella, was in his seat. But, before a blow could be thrown, there was a cry of "Police!" and everybody scattered. The would-be pugilists ended up sharing a ham and egg breakfast in a nearby farmhouse.

But there were no such interruptions when the duo met again on May 1, 1889, at Marshfield, on the county boundary between Glamorgan and Monmouthshire. Shoni's Welsh middleweight crown was at stake, along with £100, but the Rhondda man seemed to lack enthusiasm for the task, especially after the preliminary coin toss had left him facing the rising sun. It lasted just 23 minutes – although the champion's willingness to go down from almost every punch meant that included 19 rounds – before the Cardiffian was declared the victor.

The law arrived soon afterwards, both men later being bound over to keep the peace.

Shoni had no answer to the body shots of 50-year-old Bill Samuels in a circus tent in Neath and was knocked out in the third session, only boxing sporadically from then on.

But he was a key figure in a skirmish when Jack Scarrott took his booth to Ferndale. A collection was organised for a mountain fighter fallen on hard times and trouble flared when someone was spotted removing a shilling tossed in by another well-wisher.

Dai Brawd, a well-known bareknuckle practitioner, hit one of the booth men. Shoni took exception and upbraided Dai, who promptly vowed that he would get the same treatment. As the pair came together, almost every man in the place piled in, wrecking the booth in an all-out riot. What happened to the cap with the cash, who knows?

Jack Jones contracted erysipelas – an infectious skin disease, also known as St Anthony's Fire – after cutting his head badly in a fall in Cardiff's St Mary Street on Boxing Night, 1893. He died a few weeks later, at the age of 31, his mother at his bedside, in his lodgings in nearby Havelock Street.

JOHNNY JONES
(1903–1986)

- Welsh Flyweight Champion 1924–25

Johnny Jones

If you're called Johnny Jones in Wales, it's never going to be enough. You must have some tag to distinguish you from all the others. One such youngster became known as Jones 'The Moel', from the Pentre street where he grew up.

And he was soon standing out from all his namesakes for another reason. His precocious ability in the ring had observers labelling him "the second Jimmy Wilde", who indeed endorsed the idea that this was his natural successor. That other Welsh legend, Jim Driscoll, described the 18-year-old as "the most finished little boxer I've seen for years", though suggesting that he needed to grow.

The boy took him seriously. He scaled just 7st 4lb when he outpointed Glaswegian Willie Woods before the toffs at the National Sporting Club, but had added four and a half pounds when he returned six weeks later to see off another Scot, Charlie Ross, although the *Boxing* reporter lamented that he had changed from trying to emulate Driscoll to mimicking the "uncopiable" Wilde.

Jones fell at the first hurdle of a tournament to decide the Welsh fly champion, although his scheduled six-rounder with Ferndale's Eddie Harris at Llwynypia Baths was close enough for the pair to be asked to box an extra session before Harris's arm was raised.

But most of his action by now was in England, and he reached the final of a belt competition at the Blackfriars Ring before losing, ironically, to a fellow Rhondda boy, Johnny Chislett, who was down four times before Jones tired in the sweltering heat and referee Eugene Corri came to his rescue in the tenth.

Another Welsh foe encountered in London was Cardiffian Frank Kestrell, in a British flyweight eliminator at the NSC. It was a tame affair, but Johnny was sharper and faster, earning himself a final eliminator at the same venue on March 10, 1924, against Scottish champion Elky Clark.

Jones was heavily reliant on the jab, but Clark defended it well and had the harder punch. In the eighth a right floored Johnny and a second knockdown followed almost immediately, although the Welshman managed to survive the round. Elky increased the pace in the closing stages to guarantee the decision and went on to halt Plymouth's Kid Kelly and capture the Lonsdale Belt relinquished by Wilde.

Another vacant title did come Johnny's way, however. He met Abertillery's Gus Legge for the Welsh fly honour on December 20, 1924, before a packed house at the new Regent Street Hall, Treorchy, thanks in no small way to the added publicity provided unwittingly by a group of local non-conformist ministers demanding its cancellation.

Legge was able to make the limit fully clothed, having been weakened by a stomach problem, and he was soon struggling as Jones dominated from the off. From the 12th onwards, the Monmouthshire man was on the receiving end and his corner (led by former Welsh light champion Arthur Evans) might have considered throwing in the towel, but he and they stuck it out till the end even though there was never any doubt about C.B. Thomas's decision.

Johnny never defended. A bad stoppage loss at the NSC against fast-rising Londoner Kid Socks contributed to his surprise decision to hang up the gloves less than a year after ascending the throne. He was only 22.

He kept himself fit training young boxers and when injury forced one of his pupils, Young Beckett, out of a fight in Brynmawr, Jones stepped up to fill the breach and, despite five years' inactivity, took Treharris's useful Jackie Thomas the full 15 rounds. It was a good way to bow out.

PERCY JONES
(1892–1922)

- World Flyweight Champion 1914
- European Flyweight Champion 1914
- British Flyweight Champion 1914

Percy Jones

Grown men wept openly to see him. Wales's first world champion a few short years earlier, now a skeletal figure weighing barely four stone, carried in a blanket to a seat at ringside. But Percy Jones still retained his sense of humour.

He reached out to the legendary Jim Driscoll, grabbed his sleeve, pulled him close and whispered, "If you're short of an exhibition, I'll take you on, just to show I haven't forgotten all you taught me."

Within weeks he was dead. The horrors of World War I killed him, just as certainly as they did those who died in the trenches. It just took a while longer.

Wounded on the Somme, where he served as a sergeant in the Royal Welsh Fusiliers, Jones refused to be "a stretcher case", insisting on dragging his injured leg painfully through the cloying mud to the sanctuary of his base. But his courage and stubbornness resulted in blood poisoning.

Transferred from one hospital to another, he underwent 30 operations, including the amputation of the shattered leg. The other had to be broken to relieve the pain, while his body was a mass of tubes.

It had all been so different. Percy, although born in Treherbert, grew up in Aber Rhondda Road, Porth, near the fairground where Jack Scarrott had his famous booth. When the teenage blacksmith's striker made the switch from spectator to participant, father Thomas was all for it. His mother, on the other hand, was not. If she saw his name on the board listing the night's attractions, she would demand it was removed. In the end, Scarrott used to have someone keeping an eye out and as soon as Sarah Jones appeared on the horizon, both the board and young Percival were hidden from view until she departed.

The boy began to attract interest when he triumphed at a novice tournament at Pentre. But it was an exhibition which brought him a major breakthrough. 'Peggy' Bettinson, who managed the all-powerful National Sporting Club, saw Jones move around with the vastly experienced Sam Kellar at one of the annual fund-raisers for Cardiff's Nazareth House orphanage and promised the lad a bout at HQ.

Percy trains al fresco

Before his visit to London, however, Percy faced West of England fly king Joe Symonds at the Tonypandy Hippodrome, where a new syndicate headed by Ralph Lile had taken over the lease from showman Scarrott. It was even until Symonds, having previously been warned, was disqualified for a low blow. The referee? The aforementioned Ralph Lile.

Joe headed back to Plymouth in high dudgeon, complaining that he had been forced to change in town and walk to a tent in a field, with only a coat over his shoulders to protect him from the Rhondda rain. And he insisted the "low blow" was an uppercut which had been deflected by Jones's arm. He was told it served him right for going to Wales on his own as a naïve 19-year-old. But he would have other chances.

Having impressed on a trial at the NSC, Percy returned there to tackle the disgruntled Symonds. This time Jones left no doubts, flooring the Devonian three times on the way to a 10-round verdict. He then completed the hat-trick, forcing Joe to quit after eight rounds, and was rewarded with a title shot.

He was matched with Bill Ladbury, a squat Londoner who could claim not merely the British fly title, but the world and European championships as well, secured with victory in Paris over Frenchman Eugène Criqui in a contest recognised by the fledgling International Boxing Union, created in 1911 as a European counterweight to America's assumed control of such things.

From the first bell at the NSC on January 26, 1914, it was clear that the Welshman was the more skilled operator, forging an early lead. Ladbury stood tall – if a man of 5ft 2in can be said to stand tall – whereas Percy boxed from a crouch, avoiding Bill's dangerous left hook with ease. In contrast, the New Cross fighter seemed unable to prevent the Jones left flicking in and out of his face.

The holder enjoyed greater success when he switched his attention to the body, but it was Jones's right which rocked his man in the fourth, Bill somehow surviving to the gong. But, as he tried to end it in the fifth, the Rhondda boxer was sent reeling by a thunderous left swing and it was his turn to fiddle and hold until the interval.

Percy (left) and Bill Ladbury size each other up

Ladbury dominated the sixth and seventh, but Jones regrouped to regain command over the next sessions, his elegant jab restricting the Cockney to sporadic success. Bill was even dropped, briefly, in the 16th. But Percy's struggle to make the weight took its toll and Ladbury floored him early in the penultimate stanza; with the normally sedate members in a ferment, the challenger somehow survived the remaining two minutes before staying out of harm's way in the last and earning a wafer-thin victory.

Perhaps he had not fully recovered – certainly he was hampered by an ankle sprain suffered in training – when he took on Criqui at Liverpool Stadium a couple of weeks later. The Frenchman's reach advantage built a good lead and, even though Percy rocked him in the 13th, he held on to give the Welshman his first experience of defeat. This 15-rounder was made at the bantam limit, but a rematch, promptly announced for March 26, the eve of the Grand National, would be a defence of Jones's world and European fly honours.

Percy turns away after flooring Criqui in their rematch

Hundreds were locked out of the atmospheric old venue, but those inside saw Jones, looking much fitter than on his previous visit, lead from start to finish. Driscoll was a picture of nerves in the corner, throwing every punch with his pupil, but he need not have worried.

Twice Percy sent Criqui to the deck in the second and only the Frenchman's coolness and skill enabled him to escape an ignominious loss. From then on, the traffic was one-way. Jones's left was constantly in Eugène's face, while the visitor was never able to land with any venom on his tormentor. The pattern was repeated for the full 20 rounds.

The backers of old foe Symonds then tempted the Porth stylist to visit Plymouth and risk two of his titles in Joe's home town – the Lonsdale Belt could only be contested on the NSC's own shows and was therefore not at stake – on May 15, 1914. It was a disaster for the Welshman.

Once again the scales proved an implacable enemy and, although Percy was announced at 8st 2 1/2lb, there were many who thought this a face-saving exercise and that he was much further over the limit.

The 6,000 crowd who packed the Cosmopolitan – paying double the normal prices, too – had their money's worth in a thriller which swung back and forth, with little clinching and a sportsmanlike attitude on both sides. But by the 15th the struggle to shed surplus pounds began to affect Jones; his boxing was still immaculate, but Joe's harder punches were having an effect.

The 18th brought the end. Symonds took a couple of lefts, switched his feet and brought over a big right to Percy's jaw. It sent him crashing, but he was up at six, only for another clubbing right to drive the Welshman through the ropes. He managed to clamber back, but was floored for a third time and the towel came in from his corner.

"He had me right enough," admitted Jones. "It's no use for me to deny it. I thought I was stronger than he was and I went in to finish it, but I walked right on to the punch."

With the NSC still recognising him as British champion – and Percy insistent that he could make 8st – he was ordered to defend against Yorkshireman Jimmy Berry. Jones scaled 7st 12lb, but there was no sign of Berry, who had vanished from his training camp three days earlier. He later explained that he had been totally unable to shift the last few pounds; poor Percy, on the other hand, having managed to do so, was so disgusted that he threatened retirement.

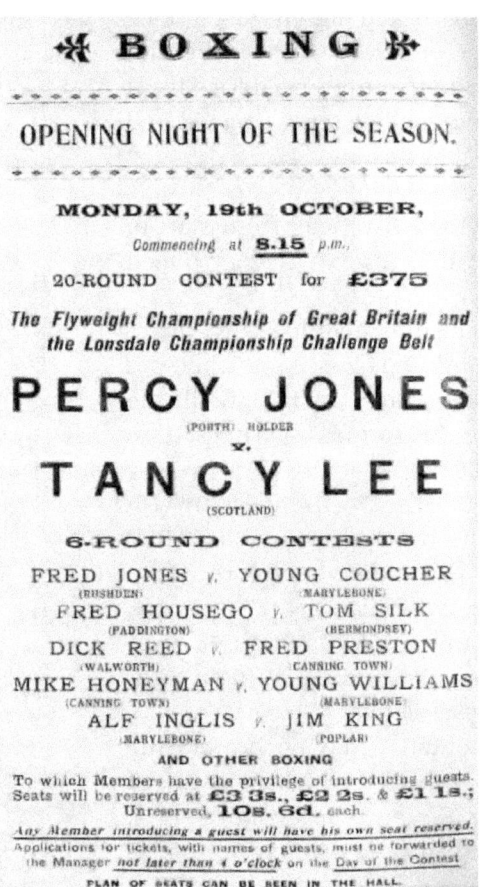

He was persuaded to continue and Tancy Lee was lined up as his next challenger, at the NSC on October 19, 1914. The Scot was a tough opponent, but not as tough as those damned scales. For the aborted meeting with Berry, Jones had lost weight over five weeks under the supervision of expert George Baillieu. Perhaps disillusioned by that wasted effort, he cut corners this time and even three successive Turkish baths could not get him inside the limit.

The weakened Welshman offered little resistance as the Leith man dominated. Although 10 years older, Lee was faster, taller and decidedly stronger. He seemed to box within himself, as if unwilling to reveal too much to Jimmy Wilde, watching from ringside, but nevertheless picked up points with ease until he felt Jones was ready for the taking.

A rain of uppercuts dropped Percy in the eighth, prompting calls from concerned onlookers for a halt. But the Welshman battled on bravely until the compassionate Driscoll retired him at the end of the 14th. These days, Lee, having made the weight himself, would be crowned champion. Not at the NSC, however, but the Scot went on to stop Wilde for the vacant title. For Percy, there were bigger battles to fight.

He joined what was labelled the Rhondda Bantam Battalion and he took the name as a cue to his future plans, finally following manager Lewis's advice to compete in the 8st 6lb division. But military duties restricted him to just two bouts in 1915: a somewhat fortunate draw with Plymouth's Young Swift and a knockout of old rival Ladbury.

The war had the last word. Criqui had his jaw shattered by a sniper's bullet, but a surgeon rebuilt it, using wire, silver and a goat's leg; the Parisian went on to become world featherweight champion. Ladbury was killed in action. And Percy Jones suffered the injuries that eventually brought his death on Christmas Day, 1922, the eve of his 30th birthday.

Percy's last resting place at Trealaw Cemetery

RUSSELL JONES
(1959–)

- Welsh Super-Featherweight Champion 1986–89

The lad from Gilfach Goch has a unique claim to fame. He is the only boxer ever to win Welsh ABA championships at four different weights in successive years. Cardiff legend Tommy George and, more recently, Cwmavon's Darren Edwards matched the quartet, but with gaps in between.

His success came as no surprise to those who had seen Russell wear the vest of his local club and then Rhondda ABC to a trio of national junior titles.

The first senior honour came the easy way. The light-flyweight division was won on a walkover, but at flyweight a year later he had to overcome Kelvin Smart, later to wear the Lonsdale Belt as a pro. There was a leap to feather in 1979, when Russell saw off another future star, Mervyn Bennett, on the way to the final, before he dropped back to bantam to complete the sequence.

Jones never managed to capture a British crown – and a tight loss to Ray Gilbody cost him a trip to the Moscow Olympics – but, with a Commonwealth Games appearance also on the CV, it was time to turn pro and he opted to sign up with mine owner Heddwyn Taylor, later switching to trainer Dai Gardiner.

Russell opened his new career with three visits to the National Sporting Club at the Café Royal in Piccadilly. If a knockout win in his debut raised expectations, a stoppage loss and a draw in his other two trips to London swiftly dashed them.

But four straight victories restored some belief and while defeats to future

Russell Jones

British champions Carl Crook and Floyd Havard underlined that the top prizes were perhaps out of reach, there was always the Welsh crown to target.

Jones faced Cardiffian Mark Pearce at Ebbw Vale Leisure Centre on October 29, 1986, with the super-feather strap relinquished by Steve Sims up for grabs. Russell prevailed in a bruising encounter, taking a three-round margin on Treorchy referee Ivor Bassett's card.

A cut over the right eye in the sixth never bothered him, although a gash at the side of the left in the last session was a different matter, with Bassett twice taking him to his corner to have the blood wiped away.

"I thought he was going to stop it," admitted Jones. "I pleaded with him to let me go on." Happily, the official did so.

From then on it was more about the money. Russell headed for other fighters' back yards, across Britain and the Continent, inevitably losing more than he won, including a sixth-round stoppage by future WBC feather boss Paul Hodkinson.

Just as victories over two unbeaten fighters, Ronnie Green and Tim Driscoll, revived a bit of ambition, he was sidelined by a health scare and relinquished his Welsh title without defending. There was a brief comeback at light-welterweight in 1980, but when a late switch of opponent saw him halted in three by African champion Kialwe Kayumba in France, it was the last straw.

After years selling insurance, Jones now earns a crust as a window cleaner, while getting his sporting kicks on the bowls green.

SAMMY JONES
(1899–1972)

- Welsh Paperweight Champion 1920
- Welsh Bantamweight Champion 1925–26

Back in the days when Jimmy Wilde was in his pomp, it is hard to imagine an experienced manager like Teddy Lewis turning away a youngster because he was too small.

But Sammy 'Sara' – the nickname, almost mandatory in a world full of Joneses, was in honour of his widowed mother, Sarah – looked so good in outpointing the respected Eric Jones, of Pontygwaith, that Lewis changed his mind and added the winner to his roster.

Sarah raised her five children – three other sons, Will, Dai and Benny, all boxed – in William Street, Ystrad, and, with cash in short supply, the day after his 14th birthday saw Sammy start down the pit. A few months later he also began boxing at the Pentre Hotel gym. At 15 he was being paid for his punches.

The Jones boy had protruding teeth and these were seemingly responsible for a defeat when he took on local Johnny Murton in Plymouth. When Murton suffered a six-inch scratch on his shoulder, the referee promptly disqualified Sammy, despite all his protests that the contact between Welsh gnashers and Devonian flesh had been totally accidental.

Not to worry. Next time out, the Rhondda youngster acquired his first title. Form was on his side when he took on Welsh paperweight champion Tal Jones at a packed Llwynypia Baths on May 8, 1920. Tal had been stopped by Johnny Broker, while Sammy had overcome the Londoner on several occasions, and to add to the champion's worries he had to shed two surplus ounces at the weigh-in.

Nevertheless, the Caerau boy seemed to many at ringside to have controlled the fight, despite a storming finish by Sammy. The inexperienced referee, a late substitute after objections had been raised to the original choice, decided that the challenger had done enough, so at least the Rhondda element in the crowd were happy.

The new ruler was now training at the Pengelli Hotel, Cwmparc, where former wrestling champion Will Hughes had opened a gym, but most of his competitive action took place the other side of Offa's Dyke. He became popular both in Manchester, even earning a decision over Birkenhead's Billy Morris after being floored four times, and the more august surroundings of the National Sporting Club.

It was at one of London's more down-to-earth venues, the Ring at Blackfriars, that Jones, by now a bantamweight – there had never been any interest in defending his Welsh 7st 10lb crown – saw off four rivals in a drawn-out tournament before failing controversially in the 20-round final. Soldier Barney O'Malley, from Poplar, looked destined for a points verdict, but was dropped in the final session and looked exhausted – far more so than the Welshman. Yet, with just 10 seconds remaining in the contest, former two-weight champion Matt Wells, who was refereeing, abruptly waved

A young Sammy Jones (left) with Benny Thomas

matters off and raised O'Malley's arm. It was a bizarre stoppage, even if the Londoner probably merited the victory.

It was more than three years before Sammy reappeared in a Welsh ring and dropped a 15-round decision to Welsh bantam king Albert Colcombe. But things were different when the pair met again on March 7, 1925, back at Llwynypia Baths, with the belt at stake.

The Tylorstown fighter, based in Doncaster, struggled from the start, his left eye puffing up as early as the third. Jones's left lead was constantly in the holder's face, but he took enough in return to be bleeding from the mouth in the sixth. Sammy was soon back in charge, however, and he came out blasting for the eighth, when a right counter over Albert's tentative left brought the fight's first and final knockdown, with the shaken champion just unable to beat the count.

The Jones boy's power was again on view a fortnight later in Liverpool, when he knocked out Scouser Tom Bailey, who could not be revived. Sammy and trainer Bob Bevan were arrested and held until Bailey regained consciousness after some three and a half hours.

Jones then travelled to Birmingham to tackle local favourite Len Fowler over 15 rounds. He felled Fowler twice in the 14th session, but Len scrambled up to produce a punch which laid Sammy out for the full 10 seconds. It was enough for the NSC to match the duo in a British title eliminator, but the Brummie's higher workrate clinched the decision.

Back in Wales, Jones put his national crown on the line against Treharris miner Johnny Edmunds in a Whit Monday show at Pontypridd's Taff Vale Park. He was fortunate to emerge with his status intact. Sammy, hampered by a hand injury, was on the receiving end throughout, twice visiting the canvas. But on the second occasion Edmunds landed another blow while the champion was still down and referee C.B. Thomas immediately disqualified him.

Edmunds, naturally, sought a rematch, but health problems were keeping Jones on the sidelines. A date was eventually set for December 1926, but medical advice convinced Sammy to pull out and vacate the throne.

There was a brief comeback three years later, but the Ystrad man looked a shadow of his former self and soon drifted into retirement. He suffered a broken leg while working at the Tydraw pit in 1953 and died two decades later at his new home in Treherbert.

TOMMY JONES
(1919-1989)

Northern Area Welterweight Champion 1939-1947

In the 25 years leading up to World War II, more than 50,000 people left the Rhondda in search of employment. Many of them headed for Derby, where Rolls-Royce and other companies were taking on staff. Among those who made the journey was Tommy Jones, from Pentre.

The muscular 16-year-old actually had a job. He had worked at the Dare Colliery since leaving school two years earlier. But his family were on the move, so their teenage son packed his suitcase and joined them.

Boxing was already a part of the young man's life. With a handful of amateur contests to his name, he had already applied to the comparatively new British Board of Control for a professional licence. But it was only after arriving in the Midlands that he threw his first punches for pay.

He signed up with a promising young manager named George Biddles – later to look after world featherweight ruler Hogan Bassey and domestic heavyweights such as Jack Bodell and Richard Dunn – and soon began to build a reputation as a skilful southpaw, with sufficient power to stop a high proportion of his opponents.

Regular trips to Hackney introduced him to London fans, while he returned to his homeland to draw with Cwmparc stalwart Billy 'Ducks' Jones in Swansea, but most of his activity was on the busy Midland scene. There were no short cuts to glory in those days and Tommy already had more than 50 fights to his name when he outpointed Liverpool's Ken Robinson in an eliminator for the Northern Area welterweight title.

Another decision victory, over dangerous Jamaican Lefty 'Satan' Flynn, earned Jones *Boxing*'s

Tommy Jones

Certificate of Merit for the week's best performance, presented to him by Viscount Scarsdale, a local peer and steward of the Board. A fortnight later the transplanted Welshman picked up the vacant Northern championship.

He had home advantage at Derby's King's Hall on March 20, 1939. Form was also on his side, as his rival, Bert Chambers, from Widnes, had recently been halted by Flynn. Exchanges were even for four rounds as Tommy sized up his foe, but the pace accelerated in the fifth, the local favourite firing shots from all angles. Chambers was in trouble in the sixth and retired at the end of the session.

Any idea that his new status would lead to higher honours were shattered two months later. Jones took on former British welter boss Jake Kilrain in front of some 5,000 fans who braved the unseasonable cold at Derby's Municipal Sports Ground. They saw their hero floor Kilrain twice in the third, but the Scot produced a superb right to the jaw which flattened Tommy in the eighth. Not only did he fail to beat the count, it took nearly five minutes for him to recover fully.

There was a further setback when Jones faced Taffy Williams, a soldier from Swansea, who had built quite a reputation in Scotland, where he was stationed. When they squared up in Liverpool, the unbeaten Williams took a 10-round verdict.

It was largely academic. A much bigger scrap was on the horizon and Tommy soon joined thousands of others in khaki. Boxing became something to be fitted in when possible, although in the later years of the war he certainly managed to keep pretty active.

It was a display of bravery outside the ring which earned headlines in 1945, however. Tommy and some other Army boxers were hailed as heroes for helping rescue airmen from a bomber which crashed near their gym, even though its cargo was exploding as they worked. A few days later Jones won the Northern Command middle championship.

He was still winning far more than he lost, but one significant defeat came on points to Vince Hawkins, a railway fireman from Eastleigh, who won the British middle belt a year later. There were also several visits to Wales, including revenge over Taffy Williams and decisions over another former Welsh welter monarch, Johnny Houlston, and reigning Welsh middle champion Tommy Davies.

Despite effectively establishing himself as the best Welsh middleweight around, Jones never sought a shot at the national crown. He kept battling away in the hope of a crack at the Lonsdale Belt, but finally hung up his gloves in 1950 after dropping a decision to another Rhondda exile, Luton-based Rees Moore.

He died in a Derby hospital shortly before his 70th birthday.

WARREN KENDALL
(1921–1965)

- Welsh Lightweight Champion 1944–49

Kids grew up quickly back in the day. They had to. The school gate slammed behind a lad when he reached 14 and from then on he had to earn his keep. For most in the Valleys that meant following their fathers down the pit. It was that way for the boy from Tonyrefail.

But a fondness for fighting provided a second option for the young Kendall. Boxing might not pay much in the game's basement, but every few coppers helped in the 1930s. And Warren threw his first punches for pay before he reached his 15th birthday.

Father Thomas, a World War I hero, had done a bit himself and he took charge of the boy's training at the Unemployed Club gym, run by Jack Daley. And, despite his youth, a succession of victories soon had the street corner pundits claiming that here was a future champion.

The influential Billy 'Kid' Hughes, a fellow-townsman though long settled in Maesteg, agreed with them and soon took over his management. Three consecutive victories over former Welsh champion Terence Morgan – admittedly, well past his prime – and a stoppage of current bantam king Eddie Davies underlined his claims to be among the best around.

During the war, Kendall began to travel across Britain, adding to his experience and bank balance, while showing his ability to new admirers. Yet it was not until August 7, 1944, that he had the opportunity to win his national belt. It came at lightweight, when he took on Pontypridd's Ivor Thomas for the vacant title stripped from the inactive Boyo Rees.

Warren Kendall

They met at the Recreation Ground in Tredegar, but the Bank Holiday crowd had little to cheer. In the second round Warren landed a solid right to the jaw and, as Thomas fell, his right foot twisted beneath him. In obvious agony, he made several brave attempts to stand, but was eventually stretchered from the ring and taken to hospital, where X-rays revealed a broken ankle.

It was nearly three years before Kendall found a challenger – and then it all went pear-shaped. Tiryberth's Jack Coles, a former victim of the champion, was scheduled for a title bid at Maesteg Town Hall, but turned up more than three pounds over the limit. The bout went ahead as a 12-rounder and Coles took a close decision, thanks to his tremendous workrate and a storming finish.

On February 23, 1948, up stepped Vernon Ball, from Cwmparc. But the Rhondda rivalry, fought out on neutral territory at the Gwyn Hall in Neath, proved a forgettable affair. It was a clean, open contest, but both men struggled to find their range. Ball, briefly dropped in the sixth, rocked Kendall in the eighth with a right to the side of the head, but became wild in his effort to end matters, allowing Warren to recover and take command in the later rounds, even if referee C.B. Thomas's verdict met a mixed reception.

Despite his lengthy reign in Wales, Kendall was consistently ignored at British level and, when the Board arranged a series of eliminators and once again omitted him, Warren was less than pleased. But his argument fell apart when he lost his title in just 75 seconds at Hereford Drill Hall on November 16, 1947.

The challenger, Ammanford blacksmith Reg Quinlan, had to shed six surplus ounces to make the weight, but started strongly and a perfectly timed right hook, which did not look particularly hard, decked Kendall inside a minute. He was still dazed when he rose and Reg stormed in with a barrage of blows which floored Warren a second time. He was still trying to regain his footing when referee Jerry Walsh waved it off.

That was it for Kendall, even if it was two years before he officially announced his retirement. Having left the mines – "I regretted that," he admitted in retrospect, "I was never fitter" – Warren took over the Bear Inn, Llantrisant, later passing it on to another former pro, Syd Worgan.

Married with one son, he died after collapsing while cleaning the car outside his home in St John's Road, Tonyrefail. He had just passed his 44th birthday.

MOG MASON
(1913–2001)

- Welsh Bantamweight Champion 1934–36, 1937–38

When choirboy Tommy Slater won his second Welsh schoolboy title, there were a few knowing looks among those who followed the amateur code. This kid could be going places – remember the name!

Those mental notes would have been wasted. Nobody heard any more of young Tommy. But there was a teenager from the same area making a few waves among the novice professionals. Someone called Mog Mason.

They were one and the same. William Thomas Slater, from Gilfach Goch – though he won his championships under the tuition of Cardiff guru Fred Yeates, while representing the capital's Gabalfa club – had rebranded himself, taking the name of an old mountain fighter.

With Yeates still in his corner, he was soon receiving rave notices. After just six wins, the 17-yearold Mason had the *Echo* reporter drooling. He "used every known punch with the flair of an old master", wrote the scribe, describing the youngster as "a cross between a panther and a terrier".

Others were less fulsome, questioning a tendency to pose and invoking the name of a legendary ballet dancer. "Pavlova-like movement without purpose," scoffed one.

Mog Mason

The young Tom Slater, before he took his ring name ...

This lack of drive cost him the decision after he had floored Ivor Drew twice, while early dominance in a Welsh bantamweight eliminator against another Rhondda rival, George 'Watt' Williams, was wasted as he allowed the Treherbert man to take over in the later rounds, earn the verdict and go on to claim the belt.

All this can be put down to youth: he was still 18 when he lost to the ringwise Williams, for example. And when a second chance came his way, two years later, he overcame former champion Terence Morgan with body shots to earn a crack at Welsh bantam king Len Beynon, the man who had dethroned Williams.

There was a lot of needle involved when the pair came together at Merthyr Labour Stadium on November 24, 1934; a feud had been building for 18 months, during which time Beynon had twice outpointed Mog. It was a dirty fight from the start, although things briefly improved following referee Bob Hill's lecture in the fourth, when he threatened to call the whole thing off.

But things came to a head in the sixth. The Swansea fighter was warned for rubbing his glove in Mason's face, but repeated it within a minute, forcing Mog to his knees; Beynon then threw a left which landed on the forehead of his fallen foe and Mr Hill immediately sent him to his corner, though afterwards explaining it was for "palming" rather than the subsequent blow.

The new champion was carried shoulder-high around the ring, while the chastened loser immediately asked the MC to call for a return for £100 a side. He had to wait 15 months for it to materialise, while Mason cashed in on his new status with bouts across Britain, even though, strangely, he never boxed in the Smoke. "Definitely a misfortune for Londoners," as one pundit put it.

They eventually met on February 6, 1936, this time in Beynon territory at the Mannesmann Hall, and the attendant Jacks were not to be disappointed. Their man was at his brilliant best, maintaining a fast pace and repeatedly spearing home a stiletto left lead. Mason enjoyed occasional success, but could never sustain it, Len's slippery footwork keeping him out of trouble. As the increasingly desperate champion staged a strong finish, Beynon countered superbly and there was no doubt about the winner at the end of 15 absorbing rounds.

With the Swansea man moving up to featherweight, Mog was given a shot at the vacant 8st 6lb throne, tackling Ammanford's Iorrie Morris on October 20, 1937, at Cardiff's Greyfriars Hall. Tommy Farr, home from his heroic battle with Joe Louis, was given a fine ovation by the 4,000 crowd and had a particular desire for a Mason victory.

Something of a mentor to the Gilfach Goch man – they shared a trainer in Tom Evans – Farr had arranged some bouts for him in Canada. Crossing the Atlantic as Welsh champion would surely open a few more doors.

Tommy had little to worry about. Morris was out of his depth from the first bell, outboxed and outfought even before Mason landed the blow to the chin which ended matters in the third and left the West Walian needing attention in his corner for a full 10 minutes before he could leave the ring.

The new monarch sailed for New York the following month, though he was held up on the border for several hours before he could satisfy the authorities and enter Canada. Before his first bout in Toronto, against national champion Norman 'Baby' Yack, promoter Jack Corcoran promised that if Mog won he would try to tempt world champion Harry Jeffra to the city to defend. Unfortunately, he lost on points, although, with the newly arrived Farr on hand, he stopped Vancouver's Jimmy Chapman in his second outing before leaving with his heavyweight hero to train at a camp in the hills of New Jersey.

... and it was back to his real name at the end

There was little joy for Mason, however, with success hard to come by in Canadian rings. To make matters worse, he suffered an eye injury in a second defeat by Yack which proved a lasting problem. On his return to Wales, his enforced inactivity prompted him to relinquish his belt and, as it turned out, he never boxed again.

COLIN MILES
(1949–)

- Welsh Bantamweight Champion 1971–73
- Welsh Featherweight Champion 1974–75

It was not the most impressive of debuts. The 19-year-old bantamweight from Williamstown was doing well, generally giving Rotherham youngster Nick Kennedy a hard time in front of the diners at Manchester's Anglo-American Sporting Club. But in the third round a punch strayed below the Yorkshireman's belt line. Then another. And referee Wally Thom turfed him out.

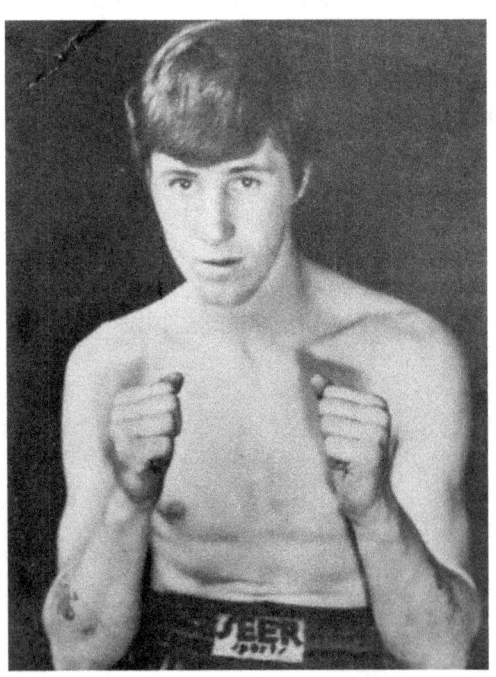

Colin Miles

But first impressions are often misleading. Colin Miles had a decent amateur pedigree, even though he only took up boxing at 17, following friend Alun Trembath to the gym. His first attempt at the Welsh ABAs were halted by Les Pickett, but the following season's final brought revenge over the Merthyr man and Miles promptly turned pro with local fight figure Albert Cox.

After the disastrous first act, Colin lost only once more in a busy first year – ironically, to Blackpool's Frankie Taberner, whom he had earlier beaten twice in four days – and he was soon in the contention for the Welsh bantam throne, unoccupied since Steve Curtis came in overweight for a defence against Glynne Davies and then beat him. The Welsh Area Council matched Miles with Llanelli's Gareth Howells to fill the vacancy. The pair crossed gloves before a packed house on an Eddie Richards promotion at Swansea's Top Rank Suite on June 22, 1970.

Howells's southpaw stance seemed to confuse the taller Rhondda boy early on, but Colin found his range in the third and inflicted a cut over Gareth's right eye, though manager Eddie Thomas's renowned skill with the swabstick prevented it becoming a problem. But Miles was gradually imposing himself, his right cross to the head taking effect, and the seventh saw Howells, hampered by a painful hand, forced to take a count of eight before retiring at the end of the session.

The Board had ordered the winner to tackle former challenger Davies within four months and he did so with four days to spare. Promoter Richards moved to the larger Afan Lido and was happy with the turnout to see Colin demonstrate his continuing progress with a comfortable victory over a man who had already 48 bouts to his name. Glynne, like his fellow Llanelli man, damaged a mitt around halfway, but made no excuses after being floored in the seventh and clearly outpointed.

Across Offa's Dyke Miles found life harder, dropping decisions to Scottish champion John Kellie and future British titleholder Paddy Maguire, before making another defence against Howells, this time at the Afan Lido. Gareth was cut in the fifth and well outscored at the end.

British and Commonwealth fly king John McCluskey outpointed Miles in London, but six straight wins, including revenge over Kellie, brought Colin into British title consideration and the Board ignored a stoppage loss to the much bigger Jimmy Bell, in a bout taken at short notice, to agree a final eliminator against fast-rising Nottingham southpaw Dave Needham, who had home advantage at the city's ice rink as well as 15 straight victories to his name.

But those who forecast a massacre were way off-beam. Sure, the local man won. But it was far from easy, with the Welshman's aggression causing him plenty of problems and Needham finishing marked up about the face. But Dave's more precise punching won a deserved decision from referee Thom and he went on to claim the Lonsdale Belt. Miles, meanwhile, went home. Literally.

His next bout took place in the Meadow Vale club in Tonyrefail, promoter Richards and new partner Brian Curvis staging the first pro show in the town for decades. Unfortunately, the turnout was poor, though those who attended tossed coins into the ring after Colin dazzled against stocky Spaniard Daniel Rodríguez. But making bantam was becoming tough. It was time to check out the featherweights.

Classy Vernon Sollas stopped Miles in the eighth as he strode towards a British title, but more joy was to be had at home. Merthyr's Martyn Galleozzie,

Colin as he is today

also a Sollas victim, faced Colin on March 26, 1974 at the Club Double Diamond for the vacant Welsh feather crown. It brought the Rhondda man his second national championship.

Although Galleozzie was to claim the national lightweight title and share in a small-hall classic with fellow-townsman Johnny Wall, he was no match for Colin. He floored the Merthyr boxer with body shots in the fourth and two more knockdowns in the following round brought referee Jim Brimmell's intervention. Yet it was the last triumph on the Miles record.

A draw and three defeats – one to future British champion Alan Richardson – prompted him to hang up his gloves. There was a brief, disastrous comeback three years later, when Scouse novice Jimmy Brown crushed him in a mere 98 seconds. This time the retirement was permanent.

BILLY MOORE
(1899–????)

- Welsh Lightweight Champion 1924–25

Some people are not satisfied with becoming champions themselves. They then set about teaching others how to match their achievements. One such was the miner's son from Penygraig.

His own career began in the dark days of World War I, and even in 1918, when he was called up to serve with the Monmouth Regiment, his Army service did not seem to get in the way of his boxing, as he picked up experience in London to add to that accumulated on his native heath. On one trip to the Smoke, when he earned a revenge victory over Hackney boy Billy Handley, the referee at the old Premierland raised a few eyebrows by holding the Welshman's arm aloft "American-style", clearly something of a novelty at the time.

By 1924 Moore's reputation had grown to the extent that he was given a shot at the Welsh lightweight crown worn by Blaenavon's Tommy Morgan. It was repeatedly postponed as the champion struggled to overcome injury and the ringrust Morgan had accumulated during that time showed when the pair finally crossed gloves at Pontypool's Crane Street Cinema on March 31, 1924.

Billy was no great puncher, but his long left leads and clever footwork proved decisive, as Tommy let himself be drawn in and was gradually worn down. Moore was the better ring general, varying his tactics; he was guilty of holding on occasion, but was able to recover an early deficit and, although there was not much between them at the end, the verdict was well received even in his rival's territory. In addition to the belt, Billy won a £200 sidestake.

He found it difficult to transfer that success on to a wider scene, however, two visits to London that year seeing him knocked out inside a round by both Sonny Bird and Alf Simmons. The second time Moore was unconscious for some time and had to be helped from the ring.

At home, however, he underlined his superiority by repeating a previous points win over former British feather challenger Danny Morgan, from Tirphil, at Pontypridd's Taff Vale Park. They were evenly matched at long range, but

Billy was stronger inside. Morgan was past his prime, but staged a brave late rally, though it was not enough to deny the "more enterprising" champion on the card of referee Bob Hill.

Billy Moore's application to the recently established Board – a licence cost a boxer 25p a year

After another successful defence against Crumlin's Edgar Evans – apparently recognised as a title bout even though Moore was overweight – he threw away the title when he met Pentrebach trier Billy Ward at Llwynypia Baths on November 23, 1925. The holder had Ward in serious trouble in the 13th, but his attempts to finish it were so wild that the Merthyr man was able to fiddle his way through to the bell. Moore was still clearly ahead when a punch strayed below the belt in the 16th and referee Hill, following the "no tolerance" code of the day, immediately turfed him out. The loser's trainer, ex-pro Dai Stephens, accused Ward of going down only when he heard his corner and fans appeal for a foul, though he did admit the blow was low.

It was time to step up to welterweight, where he was soon nominated to challenge Tom Thomas in a bid for a second Welsh honour. Although Thomas hailed from Deri, in the Rhymney Valley, they met out west at Milford Haven on September 18, 1926. Thomas started faster, but was caught off-balance and floored in the third. Moore dropped him again in the fourth and as Tom was on one knee, with his hand resting on the ropes, Billy stepped back momentarily before moving back in and landing a blow to the kneeling man's head. Referee Hill disqualified him and the remorseful Moore addressed the crowd, apologising for his stupidity and the fact that it had cut short their entertainment.

A retirement victory over old foe Tommy Morgan put Billy in the frame for another shot, confirmed by a decision over Ammanford's Idris Jones after referee Cliff Parfitt had been unsighted when Jones was dropped by a low blow in the first. But the new champion, Ben Marshall, who could already boast a points win over Moore, insisted on the lion's share of the purse. "When I was champion I never claimed that right," stormed Billy. "Why should I be made a victim now?"

The duo did meet twice, but in non-title encounters: Moore floored the Newport man in the first, but had to retire with a damaged thumb, while the second clash ended even.

Billy never did get another title fight, but by now he was managing and training others at Penygraig's Gethin Hotel, where he became the licensee in 1926. He guided Jerry Daley to a Welsh title, while he also managed Tommy Farr at one stage before moving to Barry in 1937 to take over the King William IV. After the death of his wife, Florence, in 1948, he left the pub, but where he went remains a mystery.

REES MOORE
(1922-1995)

- Welsh Welterweight Champion 1953-57

Johnny Cash had it right. His "boy named Sue" had to learn to fight and it was much the same for Cyril Moore. There weren't too many called Cyril in Luton when the Maerdy-born youngster was growing up and the local kids enjoyed themselves at his expense. At least, they did until he learned to box.

After an amateur career of some 60 contests, the transplanted Welshman turned pro in 1948 with manager Jack Tims - and took the opportunity to ditch the hated Cyril, adopting that of his father, Rees. He did it full justice.

A respectable start saw him lose just once in his first nine outings, but as the standard of opposition improved defeats became more regular and, while they were still outnumbered by victories, it became obvious that Rees was not a potential world-beater. If he wanted a belt to his name, he needed to turn his attention to the land he left as a child.

His first attempt came up short. He travelled to Swansea to face another exile, Gwyn Williams, in one of four eliminators on the same Drill Hall bill. A former paratrooper from Pontycymer, whose family had moved to Oxfordshire when he was nine, Gwyn had already challenged for the Lonsdale Belt and could point to a win and a loss against Merthyr's Eddie Thomas, the reigning Welsh monarch and shortly to rule Britain. He duly won every round.

Moore was nevertheless earning a reputation as a decent operator, enhanced when he went the distance with the unbeaten Wally Thom, who went on to depose Thomas, and shared decisions with another future British titleholder, Johnny Sullivan. He also produced a two-round stoppage that ended the career of former British lightweight challenger Stan Hawthorne.

Ironically, it was after a run of five consecutive losses that Rees was given the chance to box for the vacant Welsh welter throne against Pontypridd's Dennis Rowley at Cardiff's Sophia Gardens Pavilion on October 26, 1953. It was a whole-hearted set-to, with limited skill on show, a 10th-round knockdown helping Moore earn the decision.

His first defence came across the river at Maindy Stadium, where he halted Eric Davies, originally from Risca but based at Stourbridge, after a mixture of "wrestling, mauling and slapstick", according to the *South Wales Echo*.

Now managed by Eddie Evans, Rees was becoming a regular visitor to Wales, but came a cropper when he was stopped in seven by Eddie Williams, from Tredegar. It earned the Gwent man a rematch for the crown, again at Maindy, three months later on the undercard of the all-Welsh British heavyweight showdown between Joe Erskine and veteran Johnny Williams. Moore had to do some exercises in the corridor of the Royal Hotel to shed four surplus ounces at the weigh-in, but still won what the increasingly critical *Echo* called a "feckless and boring exhibition of clowning and posturing".

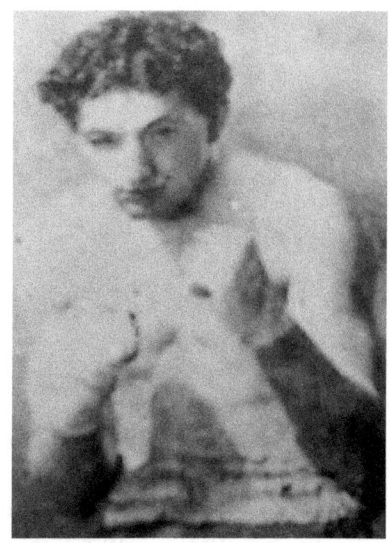

Rees Moore

Having beaten off one émigré from Risca in Davies, Rees found himself facing another in Acton-based Les Morgan, on February 18, 1957, at the NSC in Piccadilly. Only his experience enabled the champion to last nine rounds against a young, ambitious opponent. Rees was down four times - once in the fourth, after which he became even more negative - twice in the eighth and once in the ninth, prompting the intervention of referee Stanley Davies.

Moore was also warned four times for what *Boxing News* called "light-hearted infringements", such as holding Morgan's head in a half-nelson and bringing his right from behind his back. The first twice he was floored he rose with a smile, as if tolerating the youngster's disrespect; by the third knockdown Rees had little left to offer, even in humour.

The same could be said for his career. When he was turfed out by a strait-laced Belfast referee for too much fooling around against local Don Doherty, the laughs were over. Moore left the ring to concentrate on raising his five children with wife Laura, trained a few greyhounds and earned a crust as a bookie. He died of emphysema at the age of 72.

FREDDIE MORGAN
(1908–1990)

🥊 Welsh Flyweight Champion 1929–30, 1931–32

When former seaman Bill Morgan moved from Penygraig to Gilfach Goch to work at Britannia Colliery, son Freddie took an instant dislike to his new young neighbours in Adare Street, constantly getting into fights. What should a father do in such a situation? Bill had no doubts. He bought the little lad a pair of boxing gloves.

Not that the youngster was immediately hooked on the sport, even though his uncle, Harry Henry, was a renowned mountain fighter. It was only when the teenage Freddie was himself a miner, with time on his hands during the 1926 General Strike, that he returned to the ring.

Freddie Morgan (facing) v Ron Stephens at Ninian Park

And it was not long before his fists were adding a few bob to the household budget. His talent, developed under the tuition of Tom White (Rees Henry was to take over in due course), was soon apparent and when the newly formed Welsh Association and Control Board began to organise the previously ad hoc "Welsh titles" in 1928, Morgan applied for consideration in the flyweight division.

It was too soon. Although he developed into a clever box-fighter, in the early days Freddie relied too much on landing a big right hand. Terence Morgan, from the fighting Tirphil tribe, kept clear of it to win their eliminator.

Morgan finally had his chance against former victim Phineas John at the Palais de Danse, Pontypridd, on July 24, 1929.

The bout was slow to catch fire, but John landed a solid left in the third and began to take command behind his jab. At the halfway mark the Gelli man was clearly ahead, but Freddie started to get inside and work to the body. The champion began to wilt and took sustained punishment and, although he was able to survive the course, Morgan received the verdict, although referee Bob Hill came in for some noisy criticism from the John camp.

Freddie introduced himself to fans in London and Liverpool before returning home two days before Christmas to defend his crown against another Rhondda rival, Young Beckett, back at the Palais. There was plenty of drama at the weigh-in, when manager Teddy Lewis fell from the ring, fracturing two ribs.

The fight itself ended in a draw, which, inevitably, had both sides screaming robbery. In a mirror image of the John contest, Morgan controlled the first half-dozen rounds, before Beckett – like Phineas, a Gelli boy – began to draw closer. But despite the challenger's increased workrate, Freddie's immaculate defence meant that he missed repeatedly, while Morgan's own lead was still finding its target. The holder's tiredness allowed Beckett to control the closing stages and Mr Hill raised the arms of both men.

Teddy Lewis, who managed Morgan

After expending so much effort to win and retain the title, Freddie then threw it away. He defended against local boy Jerry O'Neil at Snow's Pavilion, Merthyr, on July 12, 1930, and, after weathering a lively opening by the challenger, was in total control. He even floored Jerry in the fourth, but then hurled another right before his stricken foe could rise. Despite Freddie's protests that he thought O'Neil's knee had left the canvas, referee C.B. Thomas disqualified him.

The Merthyr man soon relinquished his fortunately acquired belt, giving Morgan an early chance to regain it against an outstanding teenager from Swansea, Len Beynon. The youngster had home advantage at the Shaftesbury Theatre on March 7, 1931, but was disconcerted by Freddie's speed out of the blocks. Forced on to the defensive by this unexpected early pressure, the favourite's confidence wobbled and he became cautious in the extreme, unable to combat the Rhondda fighter's bob-and-weave style.

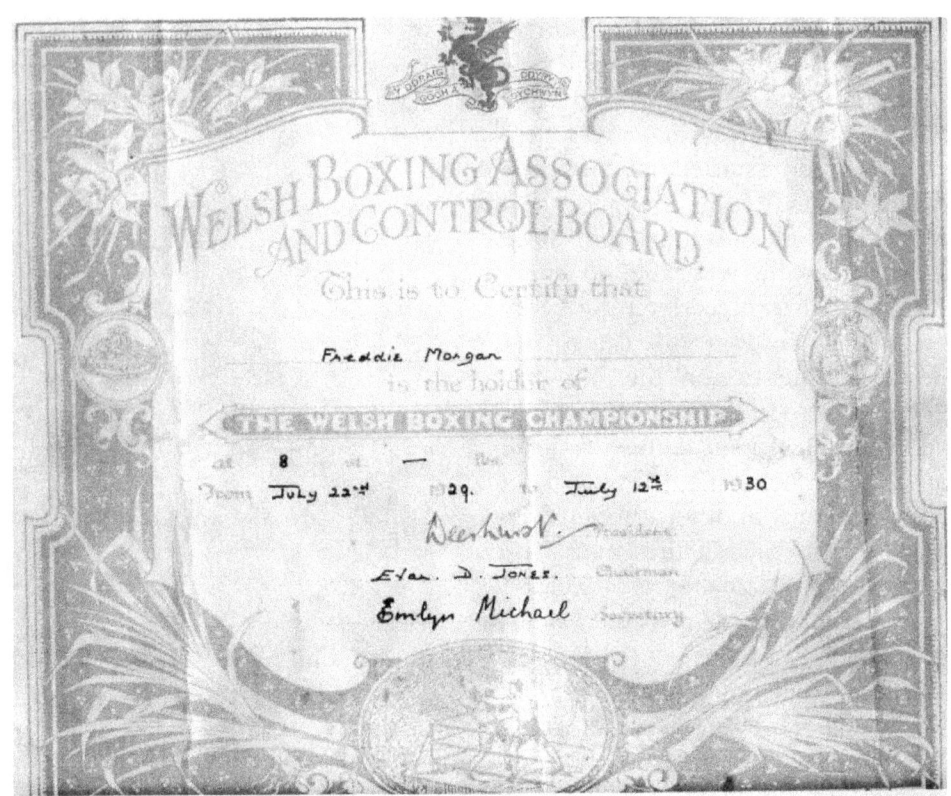

Freddie's title certificate ...

... and medal

Len had a little success with uppercuts, but the stronger and more ring-hardened Morgan dominated the last three sessions to run out a comfortable winner for C.B. Thomas, whose verdict found favour even with the Beynon faction.

Freddie now had his sights on British honours, but came a cropper in an eliminator against a former conqueror, Arthur 'Boy' Edge, in Smethwick. Morgan, who had lost to Beynon and Belgian champion Emile Degand in the previous week, had little left and his spoiling tactics were blamed for a disappointing encounter.

The Welshman then accepted the offer of a lucrative tour of Australia, only for the trip to be called off twice. When plans were revived once more, he was so fed up that he refused, prompting the promoter to insist on a refund of the boat fare. Freddie's mother, Alice, took up the cudgels and persuaded the Board stewards to side with her son.

Morgan lost his Welsh title to North Walian Bob Fielding, one of a band of boxing brothers from Caergwrle, who headed south to outpoint him at Merthyr Labour Stadium on February 6, 1932. Freddie never seriously troubled the Wrexham man, who was superior in every facet of the game. Fielding's height and reach advantage helped, but Freddie was a shadow of his old self.

A few weeks later, after being similarly outclassed by Tonyrefail's London-based Billy Jones, he acknowledged as much by hanging up the gloves.

A series of accidents underground took their toll, leaving him with a damaged spine which restricted him to light duties at Cwm Colliery. He was housebound for several years before his death at the age of 81.

KELVIN MORTIMER
(1966–)

- Welsh Welterweight Challenger 1990

It's not unusual for celebrities to attend prize fights. But the glitterati usually display themselves prominently at ringside to watch whichever champion is fashionable at the time. Few sneak in unnoticed to give their unpublicised support to a journeyman on the undercard.

But then Tom Jones is a valley boy, with the down-to-earth attitude that tag implies. When he was having his mansion built in the Vale of Glamorgan back in the day, he was not above chatting with the menials doing the dirty work. One such toiler was a bulldozer driver from Trebanog called Kelvin Mortimer.

And when Tom learned that Kelvin was boxing at the Welsh National Sports Centre in Cardiff, he promised to come and cheer him on. Mortimer duly responded by unleashing a thunderous right uppercut to finish North Walian Rocky Feliciello in two rounds, much to the satisfaction of the superstar seated in the shadows of the Sophia Gardens balcony.

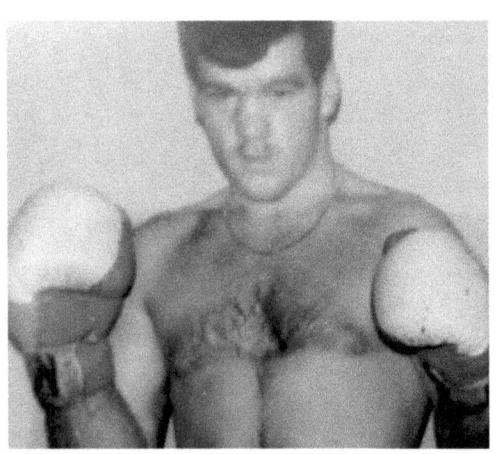

Kelvin Mortimer

There were, it must be admitted, few such highlights in the career of the stocky Rhondda man. But he will always look back with pride on his first-round demolition of former amateur star Daren Dyer, who was being tipped for greatness.

Turning pro in 1986 under the guidance of the experienced Dai Gardiner, Kelvin won his first three bouts before travelling to Glasgow to face future European welter king Gary Jacobs. The heavier Scot halted him in five rounds and a pattern was set.

Mortimer, who packed a decent wallop to make up for a somewhat rough-edged technique, would see off all-comers up to a certain level, but whenever he crossed gloves with someone in the title mix it generally meant another entry in the 'loss' column. Not that Kelvin, by now handling his own affairs, made it easy for himself. Just consider the galaxy of talent he took on.

After Jacobs, he faced five others who, at one time or another, wore a Lonsdale Belt: Tony McKenzie, Ensley Bingham, Del Bryan, Kostas Petrou and Tony Willis. Another four foes challenged for the British title: Dave McCabe, Trevor Smith, Mickey Hughes and Lindon Scarlett.

Kelvin Mortimer (rt) against Mark Purcell

Mortimer did have one championship bid of his own. He met West Walian John Davies for the vacant Welsh welter crown at Merthyr's Rhydycar Sports Centre on April 26, 1990. The skilful, but wayward Davies soon began to get through, cutting Kelvin beneath the left eye in the opener. It was already clear this would not last long and John decked Mortimer with a one-two to the jaw early in the second. Kelvin, bravely, but unwisely, jumped up at the count of three, but Davies unloaded a volley of punches which Kelvin lacked the ability to avoid. Referee Wynford Jones wasted no time in rescuing him and ushering him to the sanctuary of his stool.

After that setback, Kelvin dropped out of view for 17 months, the Tom Jones-inspired win over Feliciello marking his return. Unfortunately, it also proved to be the last time his arm was raised. Four successive losses, including revenge for Dyer helped by a cut eye, culminated in a one-round disaster against Ulsterman Eamonn Loughran at the National Ice Rink in Cardiff. Loughran went on to be WBO champion. Mortimer returned to the bulldozer.

DAVE PETERS
(1876–1962)

🥊 Welsh Middleweight Champion 1901–04, 1909–10

Back in the days when Queen Victoria ruled over her boundless Empire, "political correctness" was a phrase still uncoined. So, when a young valleys fighter of mixed race first made an appearance in London rings, he was innocently billed as 'The Welsh Coon'.

Dave Peters

No matter. At home they knew he was one of the best boxers of his generation. In those barely regulated times, he claimed titles in the light-heavy and heavy divisions as well as his more generally recognised middleweight honours.

Born at Cwmtillery to a West Indian lay preacher and his Merthyr-born wife, young David was living in the Rhondda by his fifth birthday, but two years later lost his 41-year-old father to typhoid. His mother remarried and the family settled in Treorchy, where the teenager followed the well-worn route to the local pit – and to the ring.

His first recorded contest took place in 1899, in a private London club, when he battled for 57 rounds with black Australian Sam Cavill before their bare-knuckle bout was called a draw. Peters, who was based at Woolwich and trained under Sam Broom at his Mortlake pub, knocked out Cavill in a rematch, this time with gloves, and won more than he lost before heading home early in 1900.

Despite being a natural welterweight, he faced Abercarn's Tom James at the Prince of Wales Circus, Merthyr, on February 25, 1901, in a scheduled 20-rounder billed for the Welsh heavy crown. Dave flattened the Monmouthshire man in two and the bout was later rebranded as for the middleweight title.

The following year Peters took on Jack Palmer in Merthyr, allegedly for the vacant British middle belt, though as it was over two-minute rounds it was never ratified as such. Palmer, a Geordie who had previously lost a bid for the heavy championship, dominated throughout, twice knocking the Welshman out of the ring. The first time, a spectator was allowed to pick him up and shove him back through the ropes; the second occasion, in the seventh, saw him counted out, an action which so incensed the one-eyed crowd that referee Tom Davies had to seek sanctuary in a nearby pub.

Dave disposed of Resolven hopeful Dai Matthews in the eighth of a Welsh title defence in Swansea, but then gave up the throne because of work commitments in his new job as a commercial traveller for Brain's Brewery. He did not reappear in the ring – at least, as far as can be traced – for nearly four years. When he returned, guided by Jack 'Bandy' Davies, it was straight in at the deep end, with defeats at the hands of Canadian-born Cardiffian Joe White, South African welter Andrew Jeptha and American Bob Scanlon.

But when it came to local rivals, Peters was in a class of his own. He regained his old Welsh middleweight championship at the Mountain Ash Pavilion on October 4, 1909, when he floored James 'Tiger' Smith, Yorkshireborn but a long-time resident of Merthyr, thrice in the tenth, the final time for the full count. The victory prompted Dave to claim the British light-heavy crown – the divisional limit was then 12st – but he never pressed the point.

When Peters wrenched a shoulder while boxing an exhibition as part of the annual fund-raiser for Cardiff's Nazareth House orphanage, it required specialist treatment, but he still challenged Rhondda rival Tom Thomas, then wearing the middleweight Lonsdale Belt. 'Tom Farmer' had his own medical problems and the issue was put on the back burner.

While waiting to meet Tom, Dave turned to another Thomas: Dai, a Cardiff-born Londoner who campaigned as George West. Peters was dropped in the 11th, thought he heard the gong and turned for his corner; West hurled himself at an unprotected target and landed hard and often enough for the referee to stop it.

The Treorchy man – though by now married and living in Llantwit Major – angrily demanded a rematch and they met again, with double the money at stake, before 5,000 fans at Caerphilly's Virginia Park. Peters's Welsh title was also up for grabs; for the first bout, West had come in a pound overweight.

Once more a bizarre sequence of events wrecked Dave's hopes. After he felled West in the opening session, someone called "Time!" and both sets of seconds climbed through the ropes before the timekeeper could protest that the voice had not been his. When the action was eventually resumed, West had recovered enough to survive the remaining seconds.

Peters broke George's nose in the third with a big right, but then stumbled and fell, his opponent crashing down on top of him, an incident which so weakened the Rhondda man that when he walked on to an overarm right in the fourth, he lacked the strength to beat the count.

The losses meant a preliminary contract signed with Tom Thomas was torn up and Dave sought a third meeting with West, only to be struck down by a virulent form of influenza, which left him incapacitated for two months. Apart from occasional exhibitions, it effectively ended his career, although he stayed in the sport as a respected trainer.

His loyalty to Brain's, for whom he also worked as a tester, led to him taking over as licensee of the Gwaelodygarth Inn, later moving to Tongwynlais, where he was mine host at both the Lewis Arms and the Old Ton. He stayed in the village until his death in 1962, at the age of 86.

LEWIS REES
(1989-)

- Welsh Welterweight Champion 2013-14

Sometimes it's just not worth the candle. From the outside it seems as though a young boxer, already a champion and unbeaten as a pro following a stellar amateur career, is inexorably headed for the big time. But behind the scenes, the stresses and sacrifices have taken their toll.

Lewis Rees, widely tipped to end the long wait for a new fistic hero for the Rhondda, was never really in love with the sport. When he sleepwalked to a six-round points loss in Sheffield against Lancastrian journeyman William Warburton it confirmed a decision already taking shape in his mind. So he called it a day.

Although his father, grandfather and great-grandfather had all boxed - Dad Emlyn wanted to turn pro, but a retina problem denied him a licence - it was watching Joe Calzaghe on TV that prompted Lewis, a winger good enough to have trials with Cardiff City, to turn to the ring himself.

Guided by his father and veteran coach Ivor 'Pete' Bartlett at Rhondda ABC, southpaw Rees was soon demonstrating his potential. Welsh titles were claimed in various age groups, though Ulsterman Anthony Cacace, who would become a British champion in the paid ranks, beat him three times at Four Nations level – when the Irish withdrew and it became an all-British affair, Lewis struck gold, beating another future Lonsdale Belt wearer, Bradley Skeete, in the final.

The Tonypandy lad, who went straight from school into the GB Olympic squad, won three successive Welsh ABA titles at light-welterweight, with future star Chris Jenkins among his victims, adding British honours in 2009.

Lewis Rees

Rees's power sends Leon Findlay flying

Rees captained Wales each time he donned the national colours, picking up medals from multi-nations tournaments across Europe, but missed out on the Commonwealth Games when he was ordered to face old rival Jenkins in a box-off and suffered a back strain, the authorities refusing requests for a delay.

With Mancunian Tom Stalker already qualified for the 2012 Olympics in his division, Lewis left the GB set-up in Sheffield, intending to turn his back on boxing. But Gary Lockett came calling, with an offer to turn his skills into cash. The would-be manager was repeatedly rebuffed, but when he revealed a prospective promotional deal with Frank Warren, that – coupled with the difficulty of finding alternative work – prompted a change of heart.

Rees made his bow on the George Groves-James DeGale undercard at the O2. In a largely empty arena, he halted Brummie Sid Razak in two. Another stoppage win, in Liverpool, followed. With newly crowned world champion Nathan Cleverly and fast-rising Lee Selby on the books, Warren turned to Wales, with Rees outboxing combative Tony Pace and dismissing overmatched debutant Jerome Samuels before home fans. But the struggle to make weight for Pace had put doubt in his mind about his new life.

For the moment, though, he continued, taking his tally to six before he was matched with Amman Valley boy Leon Findlay for the vacant Welsh welterweight title. They met on a Steve Sims card at the Rhondda Fach Sports Centre in Tylorstown on May 4, 2013. Findlay, a former amateur international, had lost only to future champions in Sam Eggington and John Wayne Hibbert, but he never looked likely to provide serious opposition.

The first punch of the contest, a left to the face, dumped Leon on the seat of his pants. Another knockdown followed – although it seemed more of a push this time – before the bell rang. It brought only temporary relief for the beleaguered visitor, with a renewed barrage at the start of the second prompting referee Wynford Jones to jump in amid raucous celebration from the Rhondda fans.

There were a couple of eight-round decision wins, but his enthusiasm was waning. A bout in Germany, on the undercard of gym-mate Enzo Maccarinelli's shot at WBA champion Jürgen Brähmer, ended in a majority draw. Then came the defeat by Warburton and the decision to step away.

There have been no regrets. Lewis still follows the fight game, but as a fan. Now in charge of maintenance at student accommodation in Cardiff, his main focus is on family life with Jenna and their two sons.

TERRY REES
(1937–)

- Welsh Featherweight Champion 1959–61

The accent may be as Cockney as a barrow boy's, but there was never any doubt where Terry Rees's true loyalties lay. He was born in the West London suburb of Hounslow, but his parents came from Blaencwm and when father Evan was called up at the start of World War II, the rest of the family moved home to Wales for the duration.

After six years in Treherbert, it was back to London, where ginger-headed Terry first laced up the gloves at the Catford and District club, winning flyweight honours in the South-East London divisionals in 1955, only to fail the scales before the London semi-final. Despite suffering from osteomyelitis in his left leg, young Rees became a PTI during National Service, only to be abruptly invalided out with just a few months to go.

Back in civvy street and now a featherweight, Terry decided to follow older brothers Bobby and Billy and give the pro game a try, linking up with Nat Seller, the manager who had guided Dai Dower to three flyweight titles. He made his bow on a high-profile show at Harringay Arena, only to fluff his lines. After holding his own into the sixth and last round against Dartford's Barrie Smith, Rees was floored for seven and then rescued when he rose.

Another three losses in his first five contests – the solitary victory was a commendable decision over previously unbeaten Jamaican Con Mount-Bassie – left Rees in little doubt of his place in the pecking order. There were a few wins, a few more losses. Nothing to write home about.

Terry Rees

Rees's first opponent from the Land of his Father (and Mother) was Cardiff's Gordon Blakey, a former Welsh amateur champion with half a dozen straight wins in the paid ranks. Blakey duly took a six-round decision and repeated it two months later, but a third meeting saw Terry put on a clinical display in which his educated left built up a clear lead. Even a late revival by Gordon, cutting Terry's eye, was not enough to secure the referee's vote.

Another Cardiffian, the undefeated Phil Jones, floored Rees five times and stopped him, but it was Terry who was named to face old foe Blakey for the vacant Welsh featherweight throne. Injury to the Ely boxer delayed the showdown until September 1, 1959, in the open air of Aberdare's Ynys Stadium. It was marketed under the slogan "a title fight will see the feathers fly" and lived up to the billing. Blakey scored well to head and body, but Terry's lightning left jab and slick movement kept him in the argument until a thunderous shot "down below" doubled him up in pain.

If that punch was legal, Blakey's next effort, when hostilities resumed, was definitely low. Referee Bernard Murphy handed out a warning, but Gordon immediately transgressed again. The third man promptly disqualified him and pronounced the suffering Londoner the new champion of Wales. In the Blakey corner, manager Benny Jacobs, who had confidently expected to have a fifth champion in his successful gym, was, for once in his life, lost for words.

It was to be the last real cause for celebration in the Rees career. Sheffielder Billy Calvert, later to take Howard Winstone the distance in a British and European challenge, knocked him out in two, and when he faced Winstone himself Terry found the Merthyr man too fast and too strong. Constantly forced to backpedal, Rees found himself on the deck in the second, fourth and eighth, the last knockdown bringing referee Joe Morgan to the rescue.

After a 16-month break, the Catford man tried again on his own manor at Lewisham Town Hall, outpointing Bermondsey's Billy Secular, but having to climb off the canvas to do so. When he was back in the same surroundings former Olympian Phil Lundgren clearly outscored him, but it was close enough for the appreciative fans to throw "nobbings". It was a good way to go out, constant cuts prompting Rees to retire at just 24.

There were a wide variety of jobs outside the ring, from docker to driving instructor, but Terry settled with his family at St Albans, where he ran the Robin Hood pub for 28 years. He was always ready to pass on his knowledge of the fight game, a desire inherited by son Paul, now a pro trainer.

KEN ROWLANDS
(1927-2011)

🥊 Welsh Light-Heavyweight Champion 1953, 1955-56

The two families had always been close. The Rowlands tribe lived in James Street, Maerdy, while the Moores were just around the corner in Edward Street. In due course David Rowlands married Irene Moore. And they produced young Ken.

When the recession hit Wales in the 1930s, the whole bunch headed for Luton, where work was more easily available. Schoolboy Kenneth Moore Rowlands – notice the middle name in honour of his mother – joined the exodus. And it was in the Bedfordshire town that he began to box.

His uncle, Cyril Moore (by now calling himself Rees), was already campaigning as an amateur and Ken, only five years younger despite the generational gap, soon followed suit. He was also a decent footballer, representing Luton Colts, but a cartilage injury while in the army ended that dream. Life as a soldier in the years after World War II did, however, provide plenty of opportunity to box.

Back in civvy street, he opted to turn pro – his uncle had done so a few months earlier – and after beginning with a first-round demolition job he built up a 10-fight winning streak without ever leaving his part of the Home Counties. The last came at some cost: a first-round knockdown by a former Irish amateur star named Paddy Swaine broke Ken's jaw in three places. He battled on to take the decision, but it was six months before he boxed again.

Rowlands's return came in his first appearance in his homeland – and it brought his first defeat. He took on Koffi Kiteman, from Ghana - or the Gold Coast, as it then was - but living in Wales,

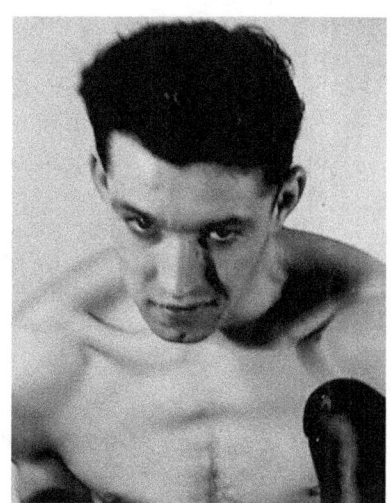

Ken Rowlands

at Abergavenny's Market Hall and should have been far too good. But the African wore him down and Ken's retirement at the end of the third may have been prompted by more than the announced hand injury.

He was back three months later to face Ron Cooper in an eliminator for the Welsh middleweight title at Maesteg. The Pyle man dominated the early exchanges: his punching power had Rowlands on the floor twice in the third, prompting a tactical rethink which saw the visitor operate at long range behind an accurate straight left. Cooper was never able to regain control and Ken collected the verdict after 10 hard-fought rounds.

There was still a final eliminator to negotiate. This time it was nearer to Rowlands's patch, with Tredegar product Des Jones travelling to Bedford for the 12-rounder. The taller Rowlands soon established mastery and a two-fisted barrage in the tenth put Jones on the deck. Ken took the verdict, but never had his title shot – at least, not at middleweight.

It was the vacant light-heavy throne at stake when he faced Nantymoel's Nick Fisher at Sophia Gardens on April 27, 1953. Fisher, four months older, had been campaigning at heavy, while Ken scaled a mere 11st 11lb, but the weight difference was never an issue. The returning exile simply outboxed Nick, that elegant left rarely out of his face, and a seventh-round assault saw Fisher tumble over the middle rope on to the ring apron. He was able to resume at the count of four, but the interval brought his withdrawal.

Rowlands did not have long to glory in his new status. Four months later he was in Porthcawl to defend against Dave Williams, a former butcher's boy from Barry, once again conceding more than half a stone. This time it mattered. Ken's skill was no match for the stocky challenger's strength and power, a right to the body sending him crashing in the fifth. He scrambled to his feet, but marginally too late.

When Ken was counted out after being knocked through the ropes by future British title challenger Arthur Howard, it looked as if his career was approaching its close. But on October 10, 1955, he was contesting his old title again. Facing him across the Sophia Gardens ring was former Olympian Terry Gooding, 12 straight wins behind him as a pro, and clearly expected to pick up the vacant crown. But he was decked in the fourth before a clash of heads left him so badly bloodied that hostilities were halted at the end of the sixth.

Rowlands's second reign lasted seven months, but again his first defence proved his last. Newport's Noel Trigg was also cut-prone, but there was no blood around at the Maindy Stadium, where, after "12 rounds of stertorous moiling and spoiling", as *Boxing News* put it, Trigg was named the new champion.

Ken carried on for another couple of years before finally hanging up the gloves.

NEIL SWAIN
(1971–)

- Commonwealth Super-Bantamweight Champion 1995, 1996–97
- British Super-Bantamweight Challenger 1997

Neil Swain's confrontations took place in nightclubs and dark alleys as often as in the glare of television lights. That he achieved so much in a fractured career is testament to his innate talent.

The wiry youngster from Gilfach Goch always had to fight. As a mixed-race boy in a community where skins were almost uniformly white, it was a necessity for survival. But there was boxing in the family and, as a nine-year-old tearaway, he was taken to see Ken McCann, the larger-than-life coach of Gilfach Goch ABC, in the search for direction.

Outside distractions interrupted his junior years, but as a senior he demonstrated what he could do, winning a Welsh ABA flyweight title in 1992. Two months later, however, Neil misbehaved on an international trip to Bavaria and was promptly banned sine die. It was the signal to turn pro with manager-of-the-moment Dai Gardiner.

In keeping with a life in which nothing ever came easily, Swain's first five paid bouts were all against unbeaten opponents. The first four were outpointed, including French Olympian Philippe Desavoyé in Paris. Next up was Barry Jones, a former amateur star from Cardiff.

'Emma' was a late replacement against Jones, who was eight pounds heavier, but caused problems with his southpaw leads before the future WBO super-feather king eventually settled and took referee Roddy Evans's vote.

A defeat can often open more doors than a victory. Suddenly, foes frightened off by the Rhondda boy's early successes were more willing to talk business.

Neil Swain

And Neil was able to face the sort of opponent other prospects learned from, duly collecting his first stoppages before an unexpected shock when Irishman Vince Feeney outscored Neil – and three more defeats were to follow as he was once again matched with champions-in-waiting. Swain floored future WBU boss Peter Culshaw, but still lost the decision in front of his rival's Liverpool fans. The other two setbacks involved further Welsh dissatisfaction with the referees.

The first, in Bristol, saw Swain tackle Yorkshireman Paul Ingle, a former Olympic representative who was the latest apple of promoter Frank Maloney's eye. Neil briefly touched down in the opener, but had Ingle taking a count in the second, underlining his control of matters. Then, in the fourth, Paul swung a right hand that landed so low it almost became entangled in Swain's bootlaces. Third man Denzil Lewis attempted to pull the anguished Welshman to his feet, suggesting that he knew the blow had been illegal, but after more than a minute had elapsed, with Neil still on the canvas, he raised Ingle's arm, the MC announcing that Swain had "failed to beat the count".

An aggrieved Neil then headed for London's York Hall and a rough, tough Puerto Rican, José López, who probably knew nothing of the events in Bristol, but targeted the Swain body anyway. His accuracy was no better than that of Ingle, and, after a fourth round in which the Welshman had been floored by a

Swain moves in on Richie Wenton

flagrant low blow – referee Keith Walker, bizarrely, neither took up the count nor warned the visitor – his corner understandably pulled him out. Ingle and López both went on to win world titles. Swain headed back to Wales and some friendlier opposition.

Six straight victories in Cardiff, including a retirement win over British super-bantam king Richie Wenton, led Swain to a crack at the newly created Commonwealth championship at 8st 10lb.

In the other corner at Llanelli Sports Centre on April 12, 1995, was Mike Parris, a much travelled Guyanese who had already had an unsuccessful tilt at the bantam belt. 'Emma' had never been beyond six rounds, while the import had taken part in 14 title bouts. But he was 37, positively geriatric for a campaigner among the lighter weights.

Swain began quickly and maintained his dominance despite the spoiling tactics of the cagey veteran, whose nose bled profusely from an early stage. Eventually it became so one-sided that namesake referee Dave Parris – "No relation," as the big, white official laughed, with a nod towards to the small, black boxer – stepped in to end matters in the tenth. Neither the loser's father nor his wife, who shared corner duties, had any complaints.

There was a straightforward defence in Bristol against shaven-headed bricklayer Tony Falcone, from Chippenham, who was despatched in five, before Swain and Gardiner headed to South Africa for a non-title 10-rounder against local prospect Anton Gilmore. The iron-jawed local survived early pressure and eventually emerged with an unanimous verdict.

But there was worse to come. Normally, in such circumstances, the boxers are said vaguely to have "made the agreed weight", but this time the actual poundages had been announced, Neil scaling 8st 10lb, Gilmore two pounds less. Having lost to another Commonwealth boxer at the super-bantam limit, the Welshman was promptly stripped of his title, which was declared vacant.

Swain was given the chance to recover his lost property, facing Tasmanian Nathan Sting, an Australian champion at two weights, at the Welsh Institute of Sport on February 13, 1996. Having his ringwalk accompanied by the theme tune from *Neighbours* probably did

Neil has his arm raised by referee Wynford Jones

little to encourage Sting, but it was the speed and variety of the Welshman's combinations which seriously sapped the visitor's self-belief. Nathan always looked likely to last the course, but was way behind on John Coyle's card.

Instead of cashing in on his renewed status, Neil virtually disappeared until taking on unbeaten local Michael Brodie for the vacant British super-bantam crown on March 22, 1997, at Wythenshawe Forum, a rundown venue on an equally decrepit Manchester estate.

Swain staggered his man in the opener and dropped him in the fourth, but the 22-year-old from the rough Miles Platting district was as hard as nails and gradually worked his way into the fight. Neil's inactivity – and he was never overfond of training, even when fighting frequently – began to tell, particularly when Brodie turned his attention to the body. Down in the fifth, though referee Roy Francis ruled it a slip, Neil then needed a 20-second breather to recover from a shot south of the border.

But he dug deep and matched Michael blow for blow in a tremendous tussle. Never averse to a little showboating, Swain's reaction to shipping a solid left hook in the sixth was to drop his hands, take another two punches and then laugh.

Even into the tenth, supremacy was swaying back and forth. Then came the decisive moment. Swain missed with a left hook and moved straight on to a thunderous right coming the other way. His body hung for a moment in mid-air, its owner already unconscious, before crashing to the canvas. Mr Francis immediately removed his mouthpiece as paramedics – and, unfortunately, some of Brodie's over-enthusiastic followers – leapt into the ring. Happily, the Rhondda man recovered almost instantly and smilingly congratulated his conqueror.

Although the Commonwealth title had not been on the line, it was, as after the Gilmore defeat, declared vacant. And, though it was not clear at the time, one of the best knockout blows in recent years had also brought to a close Neil's colourful career.

Within months he was imprisoned for assault. The day after his release, he was attacked at a disco. The following year two youths leapt from a car and stabbed him in the back. His flirtation with heroin developed into a full-blown relationship and there were more spells in jail.

The battles with his demons have continued down the years. Even his sparring sessions with the youngsters at his old club were ended when his left hand was badly damaged in an argument with a pub window.

But, for all the problems in his life – many of them, he would admit, his own fault – Neil Swain deserves to be remembered as one of the Rhondda's best boxers since the war.

TOM THOMAS
(1880–1911)

British Middleweight Champion 1906–1910

The farm boy always wanted to box. His father took the opposite stance. When the pair went down the hill to watch events at Jack Scarrott's famed booth, Lewis Thomas made a point of telling the showman, "Never let this boy of mine put on the gloves."

But Tom slipped away from the parental gaze to try out with the resident boxers and did well enough to accompany the booth to Pontycymmer, where he was challenged by a muscular mountain fighter. Tom was doubtful, but encouragement from the legendary Jim Driscoll sent him out for his first round in the ring. After he had survived the first instalment, Scarrott told him to slip the charging giant and use his right, as they had been teaching him. He did so – and it was all over.

The news quickly reached Dad, whose anger was soothed when Scarrott and Driscoll convinced him that he had sired a future champion. And so it proved.

Thomas John Thomas was actually born at Glynarthen, the Cardiganshire home of his mother, Hannah, but lived all but a few weeks at Carncelyn, his father's farm above the village of Penygraig. And the fight fans of the Rhondda watched in amazement as every local rival was despatched with ease.

Tom, with countrymen Jim Driscoll (left) and Freddie Welsh – the first three winners of the Lonsdale Belt

Thomas was still unbeaten when he first visited London, where he flattened the supposedly indestructible Harry Shearing, at the East End's famous Wonderland arena, prompting promoter Harry Jacobs to call him "a fighting phenomenon". He entered a heavyweight competition at the august National Sporting Club and lost on points in the first contest. But when the organisers learned that he weighed just 11st they suggested he try their forthcoming middleweight tournament. He beat four men to win it.

These successes came despite a total lack of conventional training. Without human sparring partners, he used Billy One-Horn, the Carncelyn bull, to practise his footwork. He would dance around, shadow boxing, in front of the animal and when Billy lost his cool and charged, Tom would sidestep. It proved a useful skill against some of the crude opponents of his early days.

Thomas's progress was not totally smooth. Stunned by former Army and Navy champion Harry Dunstan at Cardiff's Queen Street Hall in 1905, he held on like a limpet until the end of the session, much to the frustration of the sailor and his seconds. Eventually Dunstan refused to continue in protest at the referee's tolerance. Tom was not always to get away with his tendency to treat the rules as suggestions rather than commandments.

Some sources have the Penygraig man acquiring the Welsh middleweight crown with the somewhat tarnished victory over Dunstan, but the Portsmouth-based visitor is not known to have any Cymric connection.

Thomas's admirers are on stronger ground when they claim he became the "English" champion by outscoring lanky London-Irishman Pat O'Keefe in a thriller at the National Sporting Club on May 28, 1906. The two were like chalk and cheese: the silent, serious Welshman, who seemed to begrudge any time away from the farm, and the carefree, laughing O'Keefe, who revelled in the limelight. Tom's distaste for the trappings of fame were illustrated when he returned from one triumph to find a crowd at Tonypandy station, hoping to carry him shoulder-high through the streets. Their quarry dodged them, racing to the horse he kept nearby and promptly galloping back to Carncelyn.

Before facing O'Keefe he took plenty of exercise in a bid to slim down, but it made him so hungry that he ate and drank more. In the end he had to starve himself to pass the scales and, with limited time in those days between weigh-in and fight, there was no chance to regain his strength.

Tom and his sparring partner, Billy One-Horn

Nevertheless, the Rhondda man played his part in what some of the club's greybeards considered the best scrap they had ever seen. Pat, expected to be too strong inside, found it difficult to penetrate Tom's defences, while the visitor scored repeatedly with his lead and found it surprisingly easy to land the left hook. O'Keefe was floored several times, but on each occasion rose after a few seconds, as if the experience had refreshed him, and stormed back into battle.

Thomas was faster and more accurate, however, and when referee 'Pickles' Douglas raised his arm at the end it earned the unanimous approval of the enthralled members and their fortunate guests.

The knockout of East Ender Mike Crawley was said to be a defence, while both English and Welsh labels were at stake when Tom took on Merthyr-based Yorkshireman Tiger Smith at the NSC. Smith, a former Guardsman, was hard-hitting, but limited and the champion's footwork kept him out of trouble until his own opportunity arrived. A straight right dropped Smith late in the third and when the Tiger came roaring out for the fourth, scorning defence, he was dropped twice more, the second time for the full count.

Brummie Jack Costello and Cockney Jack Kingsland were halted on visits to Wales – both bouts being billed as English title contests – before a new era began in British boxing. The worthies of the NSC took it upon themselves to establish definite weight divisions – previously there had been titles available at two-pound intervals – and set the middleweight limit at the modern 11st 6lb; Thomas's earlier championship encounters had been at 11st 4lb. And, just as significantly, the club's president, Lord Lonsdale, produced ornate belts to be presented to the new rulers in each class.

Freddie Welsh had claimed the first, at lightweight, before Thomas faced Notting Hill's Charlie Wilson for the middleweight equivalent at the Club's Covent Garden home on December 20, 1909. Tom took it seriously enough to tear himself away from Carncelyn and train in North London at a pub called the Black Bull – at least the name would remind him of home – but one knee gave way when running and only repeated massage by his tutor, Swansea genius Dai Dollings, enabled him to fight. As well as Dollings, Thomas had help in his corner from one of the NSC house seconds, Arthur Gutteridge, whose grandson, Reg, was to find fame as a boxing commentator on the yet uninvented television. Not that much assistance was needed.

The stocky, crouching Welshman patiently awaited an opening against his upright challenger; it came midway through the second session. Tom caught the wide-open Londoner with a right to the chin – "the point", as contemporary scribblers called it – which sent Charlie to the deck. He attempted to rise at nine, reaching one knee, but toppled over again as the count was completed.

The farmer was happy with his harvest. "He was neither so sharp in speed nor hard in blow as I expected," he said.

The following day Thomas was presented with the second Lonsdale Belt, while feather Jim Driscoll was to complete a Welsh hat-trick two months later.

By now Tom was suffering more and more from rheumatism, perhaps aggravated by his habit of diving into an icy pool near the farm. Rather than admit in public the reason he was boxing so rarely, he took to belittling would-be foes. When American Eddie McGoorty sought a contest via the recently launched weekly, *Boxing*, Thomas haughtily replied, "My dear McGoorty, if ever you obtain championship honours you will find out that you will be inundated with challenges from all and sundry, most of them from people of little consequence."

Whether it was the recurrent pain from his condition – and it became worse as winter drew on – or simply, as he suggested afterwards, that he underestimated his next foe, Thomas was far from fit when he put the new belt on the line against Bermondsey's Jim Sullivan on November 14, 1910. Much of his training was done on horseback over the dunes outside Port Talbot, which probably did more for the fitness of the mount than that of the rider. He had also rejected the services of inspirational trainer Dollings, which did not help.

It had been decreed that any boxer who made two successful defences could keep the trophy for life and Tom had already had a special leather case made in which to display it. Such hubris tends to come before a fall.

Sullivan, who was six years younger, with advantages in height and reach, soon began to land his left lead, bringing blood from the champion's nose and mouth as early as the second. Thomas enjoyed greater success in the middle rounds even if his methods did not please the reporter from *The Times*, who sniffed, "He is an adept at the tactics in vogue on the other side of the Atlantic, where the honest English style of boxing is thought to be antiquated and inefficient."

The anonymous scribe pinpointed what he saw as "deliberate butts", though many would explain that, at 5ft 7in, Thomas's head would inevitably be level with the chin of taller opponents. Either way, Sullivan finished strongly to earn the decision, though he had shipped enough punishment – including two broken ribs – to prevent him collecting the Lonsdale Belt at the next day's official ceremony.

"I made a big mistake," admitted a chastened ex-champion. "They told me I had an easy job, so I took things too easily. My own fault, of course. I can't blame anybody but Tom Thomas."

He vowed that he would return and a couple of routine wins were followed by a date at Wonderland with Bandsman Dick Rice. The match was made at 11st 10lb, but the Welshman was five pounds over and had to pay a forfeit –

further evidence of how, perhaps because of his illness, he was still not preparing properly.

It showed immediately. He rarely displayed the ringcraft and energy of earlier outings, his punches were frequently out of range and his usual control was lacking. The referee was kept busy breaking up the clinches, but the Bandsman called the tune, landing two for every shot Thomas got home. Despite something of a mid-fight recovery, the Rhondda farmer was never in contention and found himself on the floor twice in the 12th round.

As well as frequent holding, Tom was once more adjudged guilty of butting – perhaps something he picked up from Billy One-Horn – and in the 18th session referee Eugene Corri lost patience and turfed him out. It was an ignominious end to a glorious career, not that anyone realised it at the time.

Tom lands low on Jim Sullivan – or has the Londoner knocked his arm down?

There were plans for the Welshman to go to the US and chase world middleweight champion Billy Papke, but the 'Illinois Thunderbolt' turned up in Britain for a series of music hall dates. Cardiff journalist and referee Charles Barnett tried to persuade him to defend against Thomas in Wales, but could not agree terms even though the normally careful farmer was prepared to back himself with £1,000 of his own cash.

Perhaps it was down to his Cardi forebears, but Thomas was always conscious of the value of money. On one occasion he apparently wrote a letter to an acquaintance and asked a friend how much the postage would be. "Only a penny," he was told. "Only a penny!" squawked Tom. "I can ride there in a tram for a halfpenny!"

Barnett was still hoping that the world title chance might be revived, but he and the rest of the boxing world were stunned when the news spread that Tom Thomas, just 31, was dead. He had sparred on the Wednesday night after working on the farm, but was taken ill on the Friday morning and died two days later, on August 13, 1911, from cardiac failure brought on by pneumonia.

Tom trains on horseback

'Boxing' cover after Tom's death

Coincidentally, that same night saw Wonderland, the scene of so many of Tom's best performances, destroyed by fire.

It was suggested that the illness resulted from his decision, a month earlier, to walk home over the mountains after a charity event at Ogmore Vale. He became lost in the darkness and pouring rain and was soaked to the skin by the time he arrived at Carncelyn the following morning.

Tom's health was fragile enough without such excursions. His arch enemy, rheumatism, had kept him idle for months following the O'Keefe triumph and had resulted in the cancellation of dozens of potential contests. He was always haunted by the possibility that his heart might give out at any time, having his own doctor on hand whenever he boxed.

Thousands gathered as the coffin was borne from the farm by fellow members of the local Labour and Progressive Club on the first stage of its journey to the churchyard at Llantrisant. Among the mourners, poignantly, was his "sparring partner", Billy One-Horn; the animal came down the mountain and stood close to the house, refusing to move until his old friend had departed for the last time.

The wreaths included one from Driscoll, in the form of a championship belt. It was an appropriate reminder, amid the sadness at the death of such a young man, that his short life had been one of exceptional achievement.

Tom's grave at Llantrisant

ALUN TREMBATH
(1949–)

- Welsh Featherweight Challenger 1975

It's usual these days for boxers to have generous employers who provide them with time off to train and maybe throw in a few quid in sponsorship. It wasn't that way for the boy from Williamstown.

After a three-year stint in the Royal Marines, Alun left to help his father, who needed help with the family milk round. And there were no favours on offer when he decided to follow lifelong pal Colin Miles – just one day older – into the world of pro boxing.

Alun Trembath

More than half Trembath's bouts took place in London, which meant heading east in manager Albert Cox's car almost as soon as he had finished work. After the show came the long drive back home, with Albert dropping him off in the small hours, fully expecting his charge to head for his bed.

Instead, it was back out on the streets to leave the pints for his customers' breakfasts. "I never had a day off throughout my career," he recalls.

Most of Alun's fistic labours were on the newly fashionable dinner shows at a series of posh venues in London's West End (with one venture east to the more humdrum Manor Place Baths), winning and losing against a succession of journeymen, occasionally spiced up by the appearance of a hot prospect seeking experience, such as big-hitting Jimmy Flint, Mark Bliss and Gerry Duffy. But it was when Trembath turned his attention to his homeland that he began to make an impact as more than a mere trial horse. In particular, it was a cracking eight-rounder at the Club Double Diamond, Caerphilly, which raised the odd eyebrow, Alun claiming a clear-cut verdict over the highly rated Les Pickett.

It earned him a crack at the Welsh feather throne vacated by stablemate Miles, with Llanelli's Glynne Davies booked for the other corner. But the veteran twisted a knee in training and had to pull out, meaning a late call-up for old foe Pickett. Their rematch was also on familiar territory for Alun, in front of the dinner-jacketed clientèle of the National Sporting Club in Piccadilly's Café Royal, on November 10, 1975.

Pickett began well, landing some decent rights in the third, but Alun came back in the fourth, bringing blood pouring from Les's nose for the rest of the bout. Trembath was also shedding the red stuff after entering the ring with the bridge of his nose wearing a scab, which was quickly removed.

Alun, boxing behind his trademark high guard, peekaboo style, came on strong in the fifth, with thoughts that the short-notice sub might fade, but Pickett opted to box more circumspectly and pace himself, picking his shots better, doubling up left counters to good effect. Referee Jim Brimmell had him a point ahead at the end.

Decision losses to future Welsh lightweight boss Martyn Galleozzie, former British champion Tommy Glencross and reigning titleholder Paddy Maguire – Alun was never stopped – were followed by a draw with North-Easterner Don Burgin. And that was that.

Trying to combine the early morning milk round with the late-night boxing had become too much and the sport had to go. A decade later, with people increasingly turning to supermarkets for their supplies, he sold the dairy business to finish his working life in a factory.

KELVIN WEBBER
(1953–)

🥊 Welsh Lightweight Champion 1978

The toolmaker from Penygraig had the misfortune to be around when the lightweight division in Wales was as strong as at any time since the war. Or should that be the "good fortune"?

After all, he held his own in that era, wore the national belt – if only for three and a half months – and benefited from the high profile the 9st 9lb men had in the mid-1970s. In a 21-month period the Welsh crown was contested on no fewer than seven occasions, a figure that seems incredible when you compare it to a mere three title fights in the next 20 years.

The whole of Kelvin Webber's pro career actually fits inside the 21-month spell mentioned above. The first two championship encounters – the second that unforgettable all-Merthyr collision between holder Martyn Galleozzie and his conqueror, Johnny Wall – had already taken place when the Rhondda boy made his bow with a four-round decision over Bournemouth's Johnny Elliott.

Kelvin Webber

Porth-based Webber won his first four before meeting a man with an identical record, Surrey's Wayne Floyd. A draw left both men still unbeaten and Kelvin picked up another win before his progress hit a surprising bump in the road. Debut victim Elliott was in the opposite corner in Mayfair's Hilton Hotel and many ringsiders thought Webber had repeated his earlier success. Referee Doug Jenkins, alas, disagreed. It began a dispiriting sequence.

Improving Londoner Trevor Roomes outpointed the Welshman at Hove in a war which attracted "nobbings" from the Hove crowd, while even home advantage did not alter the trend. Another Cockney, Lloyd Lee, who had turned pro in Merthyr with Eddie Thomas, won his debut at the Afan Lido, and although there were more coins thrown appreciatively into the ring when Nuneaton's Roy Varden met Webber in Cardiff, it was the Midlander whose arm was raised.

But, despite that downbeat ending to a busy 1977, Kelvin was given a crack at Welsh champion Wall, back at the Lido on March 20, 1978, and the nearly man of the amateur scene – he lost in national finals at both schoolboy and senior level – this time emerged with the belt after a scrap which maintained the tradition of championship thrillers at this weight.

Webber (rt) evades a punch from Johnny Wall

The super-fit Webber set a strong pace, using his jab to good effect, although Johnny landed some solid rights to the head in the third and also enjoyed success to the body. The challenger, despite puffing up around an eye, increased the pace in the middle sessions and Wall struggled in the seventh. The champion rallied in the ninth, with Kelvin on the receiving end more than at any time in the contest. He never looked likely to be stopped, however, and coasted the last round to secure referee Joe Morgan's 98–95 verdict.

But his reign was to be brief. The Afan Lido was again the scene when he defended against former ruler Galleozzie on July 10, one of three Welsh title bouts on Eddie Thomas's card. Martyn adopted an uncharacteristic defensive mode instead of his usual all-out attacks, but still whipped in telling hooks with both hands, establishing an early lead. But the third saw Kelvin work his way back into the mix, and his confidence was further boosted when he dropped Galleozzie briefly late in the fourth.

For some reason he failed to follow up in the fifth and allowed Martyn to regroup and settle back into his rhythm, picking his punches well to close Webber's left eye by the later rounds. Galleozzie finished well on top to clinch a 98-94 vote from Jim Brimmell.

For Kelvin, it was the end of the story. He stayed in boxing long enough to guide son Carl to schoolboy honours, but then focussed on his job as managing director of a Cardiff-based engineering firm.

JIMMY WILDE
(1892–1969)

- World Flyweight Champion 1916–23
- European Flyweight Champion 1914–15, 1916–1923
- British Flyweight Champion 1916–1923

Throughout history, boxers have had some marvellous nicknames. Jimmy Wilde alone had a fair few. Showman Jack Scarrott dubbed him 'The Tylorstown Terror'. Others looked at his size and preferred 'The Mighty Atom', 'The Indian Famine' or 'The Furious Freak'. The London media, with a nod to the top racehorse of the day, opted for 'The Tetrarch of the Ring'.

But it was one of Wilde's predecessors as world champion, Pedlar Palmer, who came up with the best: 'The Ghost with the Hammer in his Hand'.

It summed up the incredible combination of wraith-like elusiveness and concussive power that earned Jimmy worldwide respect, mixed with sheer awe. And it is a reputation that has endured.

When the legendary Nat Fleischer, founder of *The Ring* magazine, selected the all-time greats in the eight classic divisions, he named the Welshman as his top flyweight. More recently, when our own *Boxing News* celebrated its centenary in 2009, who was chosen as Britain's pound-for-pound best in that 100 years? Jimmy Wilde.

Given the man's fame, it is strange that so much confusion should reign over where he was actually born. Even Jimmy himself, in his 1938 autobiography, got it wrong. He said he had entered this world at 8, Station Road, Pontygwaith, but the family did not move there until he was four.

The son of James and Elizabeth Wilde took his first breath in Quakers Yard, at the lower end of Merthyr

Jimmy Wilde, with Lonsdale Belt

borough. But where? His birth certificate says Capel Soar, Graig Berthlwyd. Local tradition credits Pentwyn Deintyr, now a winding mixture of old cottages and modern homes overlooking the once-dangerous bend known as Fiddler's Elbow. Some insist William James Wilde made his bow at No 1, others at No 6, with suggestions that the family moved around the area.

Whatever the truth, it was in the Rhondda that he learned to fight. Like most youngsters of his era, the streets were his playground – and, from time to time, his battleground. Other lads would take one look at the scrawny little ragamuffin, think him easy pickings and then discover to their cost that the Wilde boy could live up to his name when necessary. Even at six, Jimmy was being pointed out, with much pursing of lips, by the mothers of his victims.

School did little to calm his combative nature. Hardly surprising, that, as he rarely attended, preferring to scavenge for small coal with big sister Mary Ann. Selling it on – and blackberries, when they were in season – provided Jimmy with a few spare pennies to gain entry when the booths came to town.

Soon he and his friends were arranging their own tournaments, with cigarettes as the prize, enjoyed with misgivings by young Jimmy, who, even in those days of blissful ignorance about lung cancer, knew that fags were bad for a boxer's wind.

But hard times and an uneasy atmosphere at home – his parents were to split up soon afterwards – underlined the need for the boy to bring in a steady wage and, at 13, Jimmy entered the world of work, taking home two shillings a day for his graft in the dark and dusty pit. But there were advantages. His small frame helped him fit into narrow galleries, lying on his side as he picked at the seams of coal, arduous work which helped develop his knockout punch. And he became the assistant of Dai Davies, known as 'Dai Champion', renowned as a fighter above and below ground.

The older man – though he was only in his early thirties – took to young Wilde. He gave the eager youngster his first lessons in the technicalities of boxing and, in due course, took him to live with his own family at Brondeg Street, Tylorstown.

No 6, Pentwyn Deintyr, Jimmy's birthplace – or was it?

Dai Davies, Jimmy's mentor and father-in-law

And that meant him getting to know Dai's eldest, Elizabeth Ann.

Just as Dai's chapel-going wife, Sarah, hated her husband's pugilistic adventures, Lisbeth, as her daughter was always known, saw Jimmy's own fondness for combat as an obstacle to any relationship. But love has a way of circumventing such problems – and, once they were wed (with the groom in a borrowed suit), she was to become his greatest supporter and one of the first women to cheer her man from ringside.

But her early wish for him to abandon the sport almost came true. While working on the mine surface, Wilde was knocked over by one of the thick steel ropes used to haul the trams of coal, ripping a hole in his right calf. It was an hour before he was found, by which time the wound had become infected, swelling ominously over the next few days. Only the skill of a Dr Morris saved the leg – and allowed the world to marvel at the most brilliant boxer it had ever seen.

Once the injury was healed, Wilde began to walk to neighbouring villages and perform in Scarrott's booth – when it was close to home, he kept away, for fear Lisbeth would hear – and his extra income enabled him to keep his new wife supplied with her favourite chocolate almonds. More significantly, his ability to see off much bigger opponents without suffering any giveaway bruises was beginning to convince Jimmy and his father-inlaw that he could, indeed, be something special.

It was a strike, shortly after the birth of their first son, David, which reconciled Lisbeth with her man's obsession. The money kept them fed when others were starving and she soon realised that he was earning more with his fists than he had ever managed as a full-time collier. When they were able to move into a house of their own – with a bathroom! – she was convinced that boxing was, after all, a perfectly acceptable vocation.

Luck, too, seemed to be on Wilde's side. When American promoter Frank Torreyson asked *Western Mail* journalist Charles Barnett to recommend a couple of lads to cross the Atlantic and fight for him, Jimmy was one of those mentioned. But Torreyson wanted someone bigger, so Dai Bowen was named to join original choice Les Williams. The pair were lost with the *Titanic*.

Barnett's endorsement reflected the impression young Wilde was making on Welsh ringsiders. Having proved to Scarrott that, despite appearances, he could handle himself – the old fairground impresario gave him the job of preventing other lads sneaking in for nothing and was amazed to see them flattened one after another – he began to mix in good company. Jim Driscoll also featured in the booth and soon joined Dai in the boy's corner, while he held his own in exhibitions with his hero, Freddie Welsh.

Jimmy's sights were set on bigger things, however, and that meant acquiring a manager. The top man locally was Teddy Lewis, who was based at the Millfield Athletic Club in Pontypridd. And once he, like the other sceptics, was convinced this mite had might in his spindly arms, he made sure that the crowd-pleasing teenager was a regular attraction on his shows, picking up five shillings a fight.

The silver-haired Lewis also began to show off his protégé to new audiences. Those seeing the skinny youth for the first time inevitably had their doubts. When he made his bow in London, the redoubtable Bella Burge told her husband, Dick, who ran the famous Blackfriars Ring, that he ought to be ashamed of himself. "He's such a puny kid, he'll get himself killed," she insisted. Jimmy knocked out Matt Wells's Nipper in one.

His fanbase was growing, but their hero was not. Despite a diet of steak and eggs that would have been unimaginable to his fellow colliers, Jimmy could not push his weight beyond 6st 10lb. But there were others around just as slight.

Provincial promoters were happy to create titles to help sell fights. Thus it was that when Wilde defeated Londoner Fred 'Kid' Morris in Cardiff on July 20, 1912, it was scheduled for 20 rounds and billed for the British 6st 10lb title. A stoppage of Scot Billy Padden in Glasgow on New Year's Day, 1913 – the victory that finally persuaded Jimmy to leave the pit – was for a similar honour at 7st. Other contests were said to be for various labels at and around those weights, even claiming to be world championships. One such saw the now former miner outpoint Workington's Albert 'Kid' Nutter in Tonypandy, repeating the feat on Merseyside.

Even the NSC joined in when it suited them. When Jimmy knocked out Frenchman Eugène Husson in the sixth of a 20-rounder at their Covent Garden headquarters on March 30, 1914, it was lauded as deciding the world "gnatweight" title. It has since been rebranded as for the European fly crown.

Incidentally, despite the image of Wilde as forever the David overcoming a succession of Goliaths, he was six pounds heavier than both Nutter and Husson.

But he was soon to contest a genuine world honour at flyweight, as recognised by the Paris-based International Boxing Union, the belt formerly

Jimmy weighs in, fully dressed

worn by Rhondda rival Percy Jones. Victories over the much bigger Joe Symonds and former holder Sid Smith earned Jimmy a meeting with Tancy Lee, the Scot who had recently halted a weight-drained Jones. It took place before the NSC's bow-tied members on January 25, 1915, with the championships of Britain and Europe thrown in for good measure.

Tancy – real name James – was already 33, with three children, but he was as hard as nails and, significantly, a good stone heavier. And Jimmy's preparation, at Porthcawl under the supervision of West Walian George Baillieu, was hampered by a bout of flu. Baillieu tried to keep Lisbeth from seeing her husband, but when she finally reached his room, she told Jimmy tearfully that he was in no state to box at the weekend. He insisted on going ahead with the contest, despite his wife's pleas and Teddy Lewis's misgivings.

At least Lisbeth did not have to watch him suffer, the club's all-powerful manager, 'Peggy' Bettinson, upholding their strict ban on women. But his other admirers watched in horror as Lee handed out the sort of beating Wilde's other rivals had only dreamed of. The Rhondda man was never off his feet, but he looked a sorry mess when his corner pulled him out in the 17th round, his left ear badly swollen and his mouth bleeding badly.

They put the loser to bed in one of the club's bedrooms, with Lewis attempting to treat the damaged ear. But Jimmy wanted his wife and threatened to throw himself from a window until they relaxed the rules and Lisbeth joined him for the night. Given her anger at his stubborn refusal to call off the bout, one would imagine Jimmy's ears took some more punishment before she was done.

Wilde (left) fends off Joe Symonds

Her influence was no doubt partly responsible for his decision to drop Baillieu – she couldn't stand him – and bring in Benny Williams, a onetime sprinter from Porth, allowing Jimmy to train at home in Tylorstown as he regrouped. Not that he stinted on travel when it came to the real action, adding Dublin to such regular destinations as Liverpool, Sheffield and London. And it was at the NSC that he finally laid his hands on a Lonsdale Belt.

In the opposite corner on February 14, 1916, was former victim Symonds, who had dethroned Lee four months earlier, also acquiring the IBU's world honour, which gave added impetus to Wilde's enthusiasm. Not that it was easy, with the Plymouth man reaching heights he had never previously attained.

Jimmy's defence was far from flawless and he paid brief visits to the canvas in the seventh and 10th sessions, while a swollen right eye testified to Joe's accuracy. In attack, however, the Welshman was spot-on. Driscoll, in his corner, was urging him to go to the body in the eighth, but Jimmy waited until the following round before making the switch. It brought immediate results.

Benny Williams, who took over as Jimmy's trainer

Symonds had found breathing difficult after an early blow caught him in the throat and a left to the stomach in the 11th had him gasping. He was unable to fend off three sharp rights to the jaw and staggered backwards, helpless under the onslaught. As Wilde forced him into a neutral corner, Joe stood with one hand half-extended, as if in submission, before dropping to one knee. He rose immediately, but signalled that he wanted no more.

The Americans had been watching with interest as Europe's finest flyweights contested the IBU belt. The eight-stone class was not recognised there, but national pride demanded that something should be done to halt this development in the Old World. Enter Johnny Rosner.

Some called Rosner the US champion, but there was no such title for him to win. The New Yorker nevertheless had substantial backing when he travelled to Liverpool to challenge Wilde on April 24, 1916. Both passed the scales without needing to disrobe, but Rosner entered the ring with a left eye already blackened by a head clash in training.

Wilde was not so squeamish as to ignore such a target, although it took until the third for him to penetrate the visitor's guard, when a stiff right split the bruised eyebrow. The American attacked desperately – he was warned for low blows in the seventh – but lacked the armoury to trouble the champion, who steadily wore him down until manager Jim Lundie jumped through the ropes to retire his charge in the 11th.

It was a suitable way for Jimmy to celebrate the recent arrival of his second son, named Verdun after the battle then raging. The proud father might have been in the middle of it, but the Army had rejected him because of "weak legs". When he applied again, he was turned down because he was below the minimum weight thought necessary to carry a 90lb pack.

The Wilde family at home

There was one conflict Wilde was just as keen to take part in – a return with Lee. The pair came together at the NSC on June 26, 1916, and this time no illness interfered with Jimmy's bid for revenge. By the middle rounds Tancy was looking weary and Jimmy dropped him three times in the 10th. Only courage brought the Leith man out for the 11th and two more knockdowns convinced referee John Douglas to call a halt. Lee's awe-struck second, George Shinn, described the Welshman's blows as "hereditary punches", insisting, "I wouldn't mind betting Tancy's grandchildren are born bruised!"

Wilde then saw off a challenge from Londoner Johnny Hughes, flattening the veteran in 10 rounds, before another American hove into view at Holborn Stadium on December 18, 1916. Despite the name, Young Zulu Kid was born in Italy as Giuseppe di Melfi; at just 4ft 11in he conceded several inches in height and reach. But the Kid made his size work for him, frequently ducking under Jimmy's punches, with the 'Tylorstown Terror' risking his sometimes fragile knuckles on the top of the visitor's head. The tiny challenger was also able to get inside and work to the body as Wilde struggled to impose himself on the fight.

Jimmy on guard against Young Zulu Kid

He floored the Kid at the end of the second, when the American had to be carried to his stool, but the visitor recovered well to hurt Jimmy in the seventh and, particularly, the ninth. But he paid for his efforts in the 10th, with Jimmy finally taking control. In the 11th he stormed out and drove his rival back into his own corner, where he pummelled him without pause. The brave Brooklyn fighter took at least a dozen clean shots without going down, but finally subsided, out to the world, just as his aides hurled in the towel.

Although now acknowledged even in the US as the best flyweight on the planet, Wilde was keen to bag a Lonsdale Belt to keep, following the example of his friend 'Peerless Jim'. With the Army finally ready to accept him as a PTI, there was little time to spare, so he was grateful when the NSC put him in with a hard-hitting private called George Clark, who had been knocking people over in military rings. That was no qualification for tackling Jimmy, who duly despatched him in four rounds. Londoner Dick Heasman was no great threat either, going down four times in the two rounds it took his seconds to realise he was out of his league.

When Wilde took on another Cockney, Joe Conn, at Stamford Bridge, he had a similarly easy night, ignoring a 20-pound weight difference to floor the man from Bow no fewer than 13 times before the referee rescued him in the 12th. Being rewarded for his efforts was, however, a bigger challenge, the authorities having recently introduced a rule that military personnel could not be paid for boxing. The promoters found a way around the problem, with the help of a Hatton Garden jeweller. Jimmy was presented with four diamonds, valued at £2,000, as a gift for Lisbeth. Within 24 hours they were back in their case and a cash refund was in the boxer's bank account.

But, while still wearing khaki, the little Welshman suffered another defeat. It came in the bantamweight final of an inter-allied tournament – the first boxing ever staged at the Albert Hall – to celebrate the end of the war, with the three-round contests judged by a trio of inexperienced military men. Wilde saw off his first two foes, but then found himself up against American Pal Moore in the decider.

Moore, a sailor from Memphis, was no mug, having beaten Young Zulu Kid more than once. But few doubted that Jimmy had won and the raising of Moore's hand was the signal for large-scale outrage. With British and American soldiers looking primed for a full-on brawl, things were only calmed when Sergeant-Instructor Jim Driscoll was ordered to climb into the ring and announce, through gritted teeth, that he, as the British team's trainer, was satisfied with the decision.

But it was the American contingent who felt hard done by when Wilde was given a 15-round decision over Joe Lynch at the NSC. The New Yorker had been outscored by Jimmy in the first bout of the Albert Hall event, but the rematch was closer and Lynch might have edged it had he not been so cautious.

The showdown both Wilde and his supporters wanted, however, was a proper go at Moore. C.B. Cochran, the theatrical impresario who became Europe's top promoter of the time, agreed to put it on at Olympia on July 17, 1919, offering the biggest purse of the Welshman's career to date: £3,000 for the winner, £2,000 for the loser, with a sidestake of £1,000 to add extra flavour.

Wilde's straight left was rarely out of Moore's face, but Jimmy had a few moments' discomfort at the end of the ninth. A couple of blows to the American's ears momentarily deafened him and he failed to hear the bell, hurling himself at Wilde, who had dropped his hands, before being dragged away. There were calls from the crowd for disqualification, but referee Eugene Corri ignored them, whispering, "I can't caution him, Jimmy. General Pershing is here – it would look so bad!"

The Prince of Wales sat alongside the leader of the US Expeditionary Forces and watched nervously as Wilde, whom he much admired, came close to losing his temper when Moore's flicking, slapping punches, an irritation throughout, were followed by a blow from the American's head, which left Jimmy's nose pouring blood for the rest of the fight. The closing rounds were filled with toe-to-toe action, with the Welshman gulping down champagne before the final round to help him get through. Despite the late scare, Corri had no hesitation in awarding the verdict to the Rhondda fighter.

Moore's camp were less than happy, but Jimmy put their discontent down to the different interpretations on opposite sides of the Atlantic. In his homeland, Pal's open-glove blows would have counted, in Britain they did not. Wilde was soon to test himself under American rules.

From a torrent of transatlantic fight offers, Teddy Lewis accepted a generous deal for Jimmy to face leading New York bantam Jack Sharkey at the Milwaukee Auditorium. With his manager unable to leave his business, Wilde would have to travel without him.

Pal Moore catches Wilde, but it's with an open palm, a habit which cost him the decision

It was not a prospect he relished. Not only was Lewis totally trustworthy, he was a man who could think clearly in an emergency. On one occasion he heard that a gang of thieves, having booked into the same hotel, were intent on getting their hands on Jimmy's purse money, consisting of a fistful of high-denomination banknotes. That night the raiders broke into Lewis's room and, as he cowered under the bedclothes, ransacked the place before leaving empty-handed. The prize they sought had been stuffed inside the manager's shoes, left outside to be cleaned.

When he sailed from Southampton on the *Baltic*, Jimmy was not alone. David Hughes was to deputise for Lewis, while trainer Benny Williams was also aboard and, importantly, so was Lisbeth, the only member of the party to avoid seasickness as the vessel crossed a turbulent ocean.

The American publicity machine had been at work and a huge crowd greeted the world champion when the liner docked in New York. The welcome in Milwaukee was less warm, snow preventing Wilde having his regular round of golf, while an oddity in state rules did little to help him in the countdown to his US debut. The fight contract stipulated that both would weigh inside 8st 4lb; Jimmy expected to be barely over seven stone. But Wisconsin did not permit a difference of more than 10lb between boxers, so the Welshman had to stuff himself with food before the weigh-in and then, to return to his optimum weight, endure the sort of hard exercise familiar to other fighters, but totally new to him.

Despite such inconveniences, Wilde seemed to have done enough to earn the newspaper verdict – Wisconsin was among those states where 'No Decision' bouts were the norm – only for the local media to side overwhelmingly with Sharkey. It was a miserable Christmas, but the invader vowed to make sure that even the most one-eyed hack would vote for him in the future.

There were no further miscarriages of justice and his popularity grew to such an extent that several hundred followed him from Milwaukee to Toledo for a match with Frankie Mason, a highly rated operator of similar size to the Rhondda man. Although Ohio was another 'No Decision' jurisdiction, this was the only time on Jimmy's tour when his world crown was in jeopardy – if Mason could stop him he would be proclaimed champion.

Frankie worked as a proof-reader on his local paper in Fort Wayne, Indiana, but even his employers had him tabbed as a loser after 12 exciting rounds. Things were fairly even until the sixth, when Lisbeth, who was having a hard time from some Mason fans at ringside, called in Welsh for her husband to finish him off – or she'd be up there to do it herself! The threat had the desired effect.

Wilde confirmed his supremacy over Young Zulu Kid before heading for home, enjoying a much calmer voyage on the larger *Adriatic*, which even allowed for games of deck tennis with the Crown Prince of Sweden. The American tour had been lucrative, but tiring and, at 28, Jimmy was beginning to consider retirement.

But there was one man he regretted not facing while in the US: Pete Herman, the world bantam king from New Orleans. When actor-promoter Rube Welch persuaded Herman to come to London, any plan to hang up his gloves was put on hold.

Herman had lost his throne to former Wilde victim Joe Lynch a month before – some suggested it was deliberate, in order to keep the title in the US; Pete duly regained it in a rematch after returning home – but their encounter at the Albert Hall on January 13, 1921, was still made at the bantamweight limit and over the 20-round championship distance, despite Jimmy's preference for 15. It was the first of many hitches before the first bell.

Wilde's agreement was that both men would take to the scales shortly before the fight. But Herman had weighed in at 2 p.m., his manager showing a contract clearly different to that signed by the Welshman, and had then gone for a good meal. The size difference would now be nearer a stone and a half, far greater than Jimmy and his handlers had bargained for. Many voices – including that of Teddy Lewis – urged the Welshman not to fight, but he would not listen, angry as he was. The Prince of Wales was at ringside, amid an increasingly irate crowd. Jimmy would not let him, or them, down. But all present were made aware of the circumstances when the MC, at Wilde's insistence, announced that the weights were not as had been advertised and that all bets should be cancelled.

Herman was, as Jimmy confirmed afterwards, the best boxer he had ever met. He shook the Rhondda man with a right to the jaw in the second, but did not realise how badly his opponent was hurt. Instead of finishing matters there and then, he played a waiting game, confident that further opportunities would arise. Ironically, given his wish to restrict the contest to 15 rounds, Wilde would have won on points had it ended there. But as Jimmy, who had not boxed for seven months, began to tire, the American struck.

In the 17th, Herman surprised Wilde with a sharp right to the jaw which sent him reeling to the ropes and through them, striking his head on the ring apron.

Wilde under pressure from Pete Herman

He was too dazed to realise what was happening as Pete sent him repeatedly to the floor, before referee Jack Smith finally called a halt. "I've got to pick you up, Jimmy," said the official, "because you don't know the way to stay down."

This time it really was retirement. Wilde was suffering repeated headaches, but also wanted to spend more time with his growing children at their new home at Radyr, just outside Cardiff. There was the odd exhibition to raise funds for miners in the 1921 strike, but nothing serious for two years. Until, that is, temptation called from America.

The Yanks still regarded Jimmy as the world flyweight champion and in 1920 Olympic gold medallist Frankie Genaro they had someone they believed could capture the title for the US. The prospect of earning £8,000 for one fight was enticing. When that figure soared to £13,000, it was too much for Jimmy to turn down, especially with Lisbeth equally enthusiastic.

In the event, it was not Genaro in the opposite corner at the Polo Grounds in New York on June 18, 1923. The Italian-American had asked for too much money. Instead, up stepped a Filipino named Francisco Guilledo, who had adopted his foster-father's surname to be known as Pancho Villa – not, as often thought, in tribute to the Mexican revolutionary.

Wilde was now 31 and it was nearly two and a half years since his last contest, against Herman. Villa was just 21, but had packed in plenty of experience, both in his homeland and after moving to the US. The sums did not add up.

Jimmy and Pancho Villa – the calm before the storm

The younger man launched an all-out attack from the start; Jimmy kept him at bay with his straight left, and, although Pancho landed a solid right early in the second, he had to take a couple himself. Matters were even at the bell. But then came the vital blow.

As Wilde dropped his hands before returning to his corner, Villa hurled a right. It landed flush and the champion fell face first to the canvas. Benny Williams dragged him to the stool and managed to revive him, regarding that as his priority, rather than claiming a foul, something that was done on his behalf by thousands in the angry crowd.

But although Jimmy survived the next few rounds, he did not remember them. The climax came, mercifully, in the seventh, when a series of rights dropped him again and he was unable to beat the count. If ever a fight went on too long, it was this one. And the aftermath was so nearly fatal.

The Welshman was unconscious for several hours in the dressing-room. A distraught Lisbeth thought he would die. Even when he came round, he did not know where he was. In fact, it was to be three whole weeks, recuperating in a holiday cottage loaned them by top bantamweight Frankie Burns, before Jimmy fully recovered his senses. He never did recall anything that followed that blow after the bell to end the second round.

Jimmy in later life

The 'Tylorstown Terror' had come to the end of his fistic journey. Nobody was sure how long it had actually been. There were no ringside statisticians keeping count in the booths, where Wilde claimed that he had once flattened 19 hopefuls, taken a break for a bun and a cup of tea and returned to dispose of another four. Jimmy was happy to latch on to one 'guesstimate', which came up with a total of 864 contests, but only 140 are verified by ring historians. The truth, as ever in these things, is no doubt somewhere in between.

From then on the little hero would stay on the safe side of the ropes, confining himself to occasional public appearances and a little jobbing journalism, while also supervising the brief professional career of his elder son, David.

At least he had emerged from the ring financially secure, although rash investment in a betting business in Cardiff cost him dearly, as did his backing of a disastrous theatrical venture in the West End.

But he was well aware that most fighters never saw the sort of purses he had come to expect. When the National Union of Boxers was founded in a bid to improve the situation, Wilde was proud to serve as its president. His efforts for a variety of charities were equally enthusiastic.

Wilde was buried with Lisbeth at Merthyr Dyfan Cemetery in Barry

It was on his way home to Cadoxton after one fund-raiser in 1960 that Jimmy had his last fight. It was somewhat one-sided. A stranger butted the frail 67-year-old full in the face as he waited for his train at Cardiff's Queen Street station; a 40-year-old from Trethomas was found guilty and, despite previous convictions for assault, was given three years' probation. It is said that a group of boxers later handed out a more appropriate sentence.

The effects of that attack, along with a car crash three years previously, left Jimmy to live out his remaining days in a fog of bewilderment. The last four years were spent in Whitchurch Hospital, where he died in 1969, unaware that his beloved Lisbeth had passed on two years earlier.

GEORGE WILLIAMS
(1908–1979)

🥊 Welsh Bantamweight Champion 1933–34

If the youngster from Treherbert fought for money rather than glory, he can be forgiven. As soon as he was 14 George began work as a collier's butty at Ynysfaio Colliery. By the time he was 16, his fists were adding a little more to his income.

His first outing, at Pentre British Legion, earned him a 10-bob note. But he showed enough ability to keep him in regular ring employment for the next two decades. Not that they were years of unbridled success. In the spring of 1929, for example, George was floored four times and outpointed by Freddie Morgan.

Before the year was out he was matched in a Welsh bantam eliminator with former victim Phineas John, the Gelli man taking his revenge with a 15-round decision. It was three years before George had another opportunity and this time a thrilling come-from-behind points victory over Mog Mason put him firmly in the title frame.

He had to wait another year for his shot, partly, it was alleged in a letter to *Boxing*, because the Board did not like his manager. Only after a change of mentor was he able to take on holder Len Beynon in his own Swansea lair at the Mannesmann Hall on November 4, 1933. It proved one of the best contests ever seen in West Wales, with little between them all the way.

The more experienced Williams – generally known as 'Watt', to rhyme with 'bat' – had

George 'Watt' Williams

the upper hand inside, taking him in front after six rounds, but Beynon introduced more variety into his work, mixing uppercuts and hooks with his stylish boxing, and the pair were neck and neck by the closing stages.

A toe-to-toe last round had the crowd in a rare old ferment and George's left eye was completely closed from the attention of Len's right hook, so when referee Will Bevan raised Williams's hand at the finish it prompted much dissent from the Beynon supporters in the 1,500 crowd. Some broke through barriers from the cheaper seats in order to make their protests at closer quarters, prompting frightened women to take refuge in the ring. It was at least half an hour before order was restored.

George and his supporters did not worry about all that. The new champion was presented with a watch and a framed photo in a celebratory do at Treorchy Social Club, his achievement being described as a victory for doggedness, in that it came nearly a decade after he had made his pro bow.

But he was to reign for just seven months. He returned to Swansea for a rematch with the improving Beynon, this time at the Vetch Field on May 12, 1934, Len took the initiative from the start, with Williams shipping regular lefts to the jaw. As the pair came out for the 13th, Beynon complained that champagne had been poured over the champion to revive him; the referee halted the bout to wipe the offending bubbly off George's back before letting the local resume his dominance over the last three sessions.

Williams announced his retirement, having been seriously injured in a rock fall underground, but another accident forced him back into the ring. His four-year-old daughter, Mair, was knocked down by a car and needed expensive surgery to try to save her leg. George turned to his trusted source of extra funds, but two years' medical attention proved in vain and the little girl's limb had to be amputated.

By now Beynon also wore the Welsh feather crown and the Treherbert man challenged him for this honour, again in Swansea, on May 3, 1937. George made the running at first, but Len, having taken his measure, soon built a commanding lead. Williams managed to deck the holder in the ninth, but it was an isolated moment and Beynon proved a clear victor. Manager Tom Partridge explained that George had lost a lot of blood when he had all his teeth extracted the previous week, but the Board had refused the requested postponement.

A dreary eliminator victory over Syd Worgan earned Williams another crack at Beynon, but few expected much. Indeed, before he faced the champion he was floored four times on the way to

George with daughter Mair, whose accident prompted his comeback

a first-round defeat in Belfast by future British and Commonwealth king Jim 'Spider' Kelly.

For four rounds of the Beynon clash, at the Mannesmann Hall on January 24, 1938, George held his own. But Len brought blood pouring from his nose and the cornermen were never able to stem the flow. In the seventh, with his charge a sorry sight, Danny Davies threw in the towel to save a brave man from permanent harm.

Williams never conceded the Swansea man's supremacy, however, and outpointed Merthyr Vale's Tom Thomas in another final eliminator in Hereford. But, although he boxed sporadically until 1944, George never had another crack at Beynon. It was probably just as well.

LIAM WILLIAMS
(1992-)

- WBO Middleweight Challenger 2021
- WBO Inter-Continental Middleweight Champion 2019-20
- WBC Silver Middleweight Champion 2019-21
- British Middleweight Champion 2018-20
- WBO Interim Super-Welterweight Challenger 2017
- WBO European Super-Welterweight Champion 2016-17
- British Super-Welterweight Champion 2015-17
- Commonwealth Super-Welterweight Champion 2014-16

If he was still around, legendary promoter Mickey Duff would have installed Demetrius Andrade as president of his famous "Who Needs Him?" club, populated by fighters so dangerous and awkward they should be avoided wherever possible. Unfortunately, Liam Williams did need him.

The Rhondda man had fought his way up the WBO middleweight ladder, earning a tilt at their world title. But the top rung was occupied by the aforementioned Andrade, a six-foot southpaw and former Olympian from Rhode Island whose ability to hurl punches from unpredictable angles had brought him 29 straight wins and world honours in two divisions.

There was no option to decline the WBO offer and challenge one of the other alphabet kings. Not that

Liam Williams, with daughter Myla

Williams would have considered it for a moment. He entered the ring in Hollywood, Florida, on April 17, 2021, fully expecting to leave with the belt. The verbal blows Liam threw during a somewhat fractious build-up were not a method of boosting a fragile ego; he knew the champion was good, but was convinced he would beat him.

It took barely a minute to disabuse him. Andrade came out firing – his friendly sounding nickname of 'Boo-Boo' forgotten in an assault of pure viciousness – and Williams felt the spite in the punches, a left hook forcing him to hold and fiddle his way to the bell. The second session saw Demetrius get through with uppercuts, forcing the befuddled Welshman to cling on.

Puerto Rican referee Roberto Ramírez, Jr, halted the action to speak to the challenger about a stray punch to the back of the head. Liam had not regained his focus when Andrade launched a right lead, immediately followed by a solid left down the middle. It caught Williams square and dropped him on his backside. The count was perilously close to 10 when he reached his feet and was allowed to continue. A humiliating early defeat seemed inevitable.

But that assumption ignored the Welshman's innate toughness and bottomless courage. The knockdown, he said afterwards, had boosted, rather than dented, his belief. "I'd taken his best shot," he insisted. "I knew he couldn't hurt me again." And the third round saw the consequence: a right which sent Andrade reeling into the ropes, still on unsteady legs as he returned to his stool at the bell.

It was a flash of hope for the visitor, to be repeated in the ninth, but on each occasion Demetrius stayed upright. And between times, his uppercuts constantly jolted Liam's head back, while his movement rendered it impossible for his foe to land more than sporadic, single shots.

Williams's cause was not helped by the third man's tolerance of Andrade's fondness for pinning his arms whenever threatened, but that did not cost him the fight. The judges' cards underlined the obvious: one had 116-111 for the holder, while the others, each 118-109, were harsh on the loser. But they reflected the reality of the situation.

There were parallels with the story of Tommy Farr, from the same mining village of Clydach Vale, and his gallant bid to depose world heavyweight ruler Joe Louis back in 1937: both were clearly outpointed, but only after a performance which turned the initial scepticism of American observers into a respectful acknowledgement that the unsung visitors did indeed belong in world class.

Unlike Farr, forced by poverty and circumstance to box for cash from his early teens, Williams had the advantage of a gradual fistic education on the amateur scene. And while young Tommy suffered regular losses against grown

Williams catches Andrade with a solid left

men, his modern-day counterpart, faced only by rivals of his own age, soon demonstrated that he was a special talent.

The Rhondda rain can be credited with getting him started in the game. One wet afternoon, nine-year-old Liam and his bored mates were looking for somewhere to go and called in at Rhondda ABC. At first it was just somewhere to meet, but as the others drifted away Liam found he was actually quite good. Veteran coach Ivor 'Pete' Bartlett honed his natural skills and his dominance stretched well past Offa's Dyke. Not content with Welsh honours, he twice won the Four Nations boys' championship; when the Irish withdrew from the annual age-group competitions, Williams took two GB golds as a cadet, repeating the feat in his two seasons as a youth. His half-dozen triumphs were a new Welsh record.

Among those impressed was Vince Cleverly, whose unbeaten son, Nathan, was on the verge of a world title. The chance of regular sparring with a top operator took Williams to a new base in Bargoed and he wore the colours of Church Place ABC to the Welsh middleweight prize in his first year as a senior, earning a spot in the GB squad preparing for the London Olympics. He left after six months, feeling sidelined by coaches who thought he did not match the technical style they preferred.

He might still have made it to the Games. But days before travelling to a qualifying tournament in Turkey he was changing a wheel on his car following a puncture when he was run over by a passing vehicle. The driver, who was texting on her phone, escaped with a warning; for Liam, who was unable to walk for a month, a dream was destroyed. He never boxed again in a vest.

The senior Cleverly lacked a manager's licence, so he recommended Gary Lockett to take charge of the new pro's career. Still only 19, Williams had an interesting debut at Aberdare's Sobell Sports Centre, as Lincoln journeyman Ryan Clark played it for laughs in a manner no amateur official would have tolerated. The newcomer joined in the fun, but remained focussed enough to take all four rounds.

He secured further clean sheets in his next two appearances, before deciding things needed to change. The unfortunate Vince was dropped, with Lockett taking over training responsibilities as well. And under the guidance of a man whose own career was based on power, Liam finished his next two opponents in a grand total of 85 seconds!

His progress through the ranks was briefly interrupted when a clash of heads cut gangling Midlander Tyan Booth and the bout ended prematurely as a Technical Draw. There might have been a repeat when Williams stepped up in class to face once-beaten Oldham lad Ronnie Heffron in front of his Manchester supporters. The corner wisdom of Lockett made the difference.

Another cranial collision, in the second round, left Heffron bleeding badly from the right eyebrow. Liam was already in control, but Lockett realised that if the injury caused a stoppage before the end of the fourth, there would be another TD on his man's CV. Instead, he ordered Williams to take his time, avoid the eye and wait until the required rounds had passed. Then the foot went back on the gas and the battered local was pulled out after six.

A few months later, Liam – by now billed as 'The Machine', following a throwaway remark in the gym, though friends and fans still used the family nickname, 'Dully' - claimed his first belt. On November 24, 2014, he topped the bill on promoter Frank Warren's annual charity show at the Hilton Hotel in London's Mayfair, against Chingford's former British welter challenger Michael Lomax, with the vacant Commonwealth throne at stake. Traditionally, the right

Trainer Gary Lockett prepares Liam for battle

Williams batters Ronnie Heffron and raises a few eyebrows

hand is the answer to a southpaw; Williams followed the custom, ending things inside a round.

But his rapid ascent to boxing's sunlit uplands abruptly ground to a halt. That destructive right mitt, damaged when seeing off Portuguese-born Yuri Pompilio on a trip to Germany at the start of the year, was now causing as many problems to its owner as to those on the receiving end. A visit to the leading expert in the field delivered a thunderbolt: he should start looking for another way to make his living.

This was not advice Liam would meekly accept. He sought a second opinion and while a second specialist was willing to operate, the surgery was unsuccessful. A third medic said he could not cure the problem, but might be able to improve matters; a further procedure did just that and Williams was able to resume a career in which pain was still a factor, but a manageable one.

There were 15 lost months before he returned to the ring, but normal service was quickly resumed. A first defence of his Commonwealth crown against Scot Kris Carslaw at Manchester Arena on December 19, 2015, also involved the vacant British title. Showing no signs of either injury or lay-off, Williams unleashed combinations that floored Carslaw in the first, following up with a barrage that brought referee Michael Alexander's intervention just 10 seconds into round two.

Liam knocks out Carslaw to claim the Lonsdale Belt

Things were much tougher when Liam put the British strap on the line at Cardiff's new Ice Arena against Wembley traveller Gary Corcoran, like the Welshman unbeaten in 15 fights. It was the first time Williams had been the centre of a pre-fight publicity drive – and he and Corcoran took an immediate dislike to each other, reflected in a stormy press conference where "head-to-head" was all too accurate a label.

The mutual antipathy was obvious from the first bell, burly referee Terry O'Connor calling the pair together for a lecture just 30 seconds in, and the rancour spread to both sets of fans, with the bout played out to a background of conflict in the crowd which was eventually ended by police. Within the ropes, the Londoner was docked a point in the eighth for persistent transgressions before Liam's power finally told as he drove Gary to the canvas in the 11th, following up to force the stoppage.

Back in Cardiff – but this time at the Motorpoint Arena – Williams, having relinquished the Commonwealth belt, was booked to risk the British against another unbeaten Londoner, Ahmet Patterson, but the Dulwich fighter was attacked with a brick by three men while out running, suffering head injuries which meant not merely withdrawal from his Welsh engagement but enforced retirement.

Promoter Warren whistled up a Hungarian, Gabor Gorbics, and swiftly rebranded the bout as for the conveniently unoccupied WBO European throne. Tough and durable, he was nonetheless no match for Liam, who finished the job in the eighth with a venomous left to the midriff. A few weeks later the Rhondda man welcomed a new year full of promise. But 2017 proved a disaster.

Corcoran and Williams go head-to-head for real

Looming on the horizon was a showdown with another Liam, the third of the fighting Smith boys from Merseyside and Williams's predecessor as ruler of Britain. 'Beefy' had abandoned domestic duties when he won the WBO crown, but that had been violently removed by the exceptional 'Canelo' Álvarez and the Scouser was back among mortal men. The WBO still thought enough of him to sanction the meeting at Manchester Arena on April 8, 2017, for their interim championship.

Smith blew the opportunity by coming in overweight, but his Welsh namesake could still claim the prize and made a fine start, outboxing his rival in the early rounds. The Liverpool Liam enjoyed some success in the middle sessions, but Williams took the eighth. Then, in the ninth, heads came together and when they parted the Clydach Vale fighter was bleeding profusely from a gash across his right eyelid. It was a horrible cut and inevitable that Lockett pulled his man out in the interval.

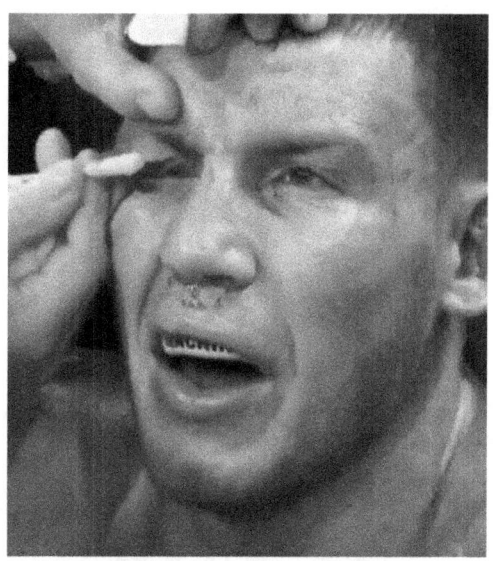

The cut that ended Williams's first bout with Smith

The decision should have gone to the judges, all three of whom had Williams in front. But the referee, again O'Connor, had failed to see the incident and, without his ruling that there had been an accidental foul, victory went to Smith. Television replays clearly showed the cause; for months Lockett would show anyone interested (and some who weren't) the relevant footage on his phone.

A rematch was inevitable. It materialised in Newcastle seven months later; the WBO merely considered it an eliminator, but this time Smith did make the weight. He also changed tactics, boxing on the retreat and allowing Williams to take the initiative. But the Merseysider stuck to the plan and eventually began to land frequent jabs, while for the most part escaping retribution. While the Welshman landed the more spectacular blows, his antagonist was scoring regularly and sneaking rounds.

After a technical battle with neither butt nor cut, two of the judges favoured Smith by margins of four and six rounds, while their colleague had the pair level. Despite the majority decision, Williams, so unjustly served first time around, had no great reason for complaint.

The defeat was a double whammy. Not merely were his hopes of world glory derailed, but the loss to a fellow-Brit under championship conditions meant Liam was stripped of the Lonsdale Belt. It was time to pause and re-evaluate.

There was little point in persevering with the struggle to make 11st. In fact, when he reappeared Williams scaled more than the super-middle limit – and was a full light-heavy for the second of two mark-time stoppage wins.

Liam and new mentor Dominic Ingle

But there were changes outside the ropes, too. He signed a managerial deal with the expanding MTK empire and, a few months later, split amicably with Lockett and headed to Sheffield to join Dominic Ingle, son of Brendan, the legendary Irish guru who masterminded the careers of Naseem Hamed and Johnny Nelson.

The changes paid off with a special present for Christmas. While Ronnie Heffron had called it a day after his defeat by Williams, brother Mark was a rising star in the Warren camp and the promoter had won the purse offers to stage his mandatory challenge to British middle ruler Jason Welborn. When Welborn gave up the strap for an unsuccessful shot at world honours, Williams was drafted in to oppose Heffron for the newly empty throne at Manchester Arena on December 22, 2018.

Warren clearly expected his prospect, with 21 straight victories – 17 of them quickly – to be too big for a former super-welter. *Boxing News* agreed,

Celebration time after Williams flattens Fox

tipping the Oldham man to prevail in eight rounds. They were well wide of the mark. Liam dominated from the first bell, his underrated boxing skills negating Heffron's vaunted power, before unloading a volley of punches in the tenth to force referee Howard Foster to rescue the pre-fight favourite. It made Liam only the sixth Welshman to be British champion at two weights.

First in line to tackle the new monarch was fan favourite Joe Mullender, but the Essex boy was out of his depth. Liam's jab landed with metronomic precision until a second-round attack deposited Joe face-first on the Albert Hall canvas. He scraped himself off and lurched to his feet, where Williams was, shockingly, allowed to drop him again for an unnecessary count-out.

It was time to investigate wider possibilities and Warren imported stocky French-Algerian Karim Achour to the O2 for a showdown that would involve the vacant WBC Silver belt, valuable more for the world ranking it would bring than the bauble itself. Achour's five losses had all been on points and he had proved his durability by lasting 12 rounds with fearsome Canadian David Lemieux. It made no difference to Liam, who floored him twice in round two before referee John Latham leapt to the rescue.

There followed a bizarre interlude when Don King, a fading force on the world scene but desperate to remain relevant, obtained WBC approval for a final eliminator between his fighter, Roberto García, and Williams. There was even talk of it taking place in Kinshasa, as some sort of sequel to the 'Rumble in the Jungle' between George Foreman and Muhammad Ali, with which the fuzzy-haired promoter first made his name. But nothing materialised and an annoyed Welshman had to settle for a match in the far less exotic Copper Box Arena in London's Olympic Park, with another fringe honour, this time the WBO Inter-Continental version, at stake.

The other corner contained American Alantez Fox, at a spindly 6ft 4in a complete contrast to the 5ft 8in Achour. The Maryland man had lost just once in 28 contests – and that saw him floor Andrade before dropping a 12-round decision in the last bout before Demetrius donned the WBO crown.

On paper the Fox in the Box posed a problem, but Liam soon established a superiority that was underscored when he cut Alantez in the third, knocked him off his feet in the fourth with a right down the pipe and completed the execution in the next with a two-fisted assault which saw the Yank slowly slump beneath the ropes for referee Steve Gray to wave it off.

WBO boss Francisco Valcárcel ruled that, contrary to the billing, the fight had not been a final eliminator, though Williams took over Fox's No 2 slot in the ratings. Yet the longed-for shot at Andrade was still some way off. Demetrius showed no great interest in coming to the negotiating table – and then Covid-19 stopped the world in its tracks. As boxing slowly resumed behind closed doors, a frustrated British champion was forced to address the matter of his mandatory defence against Andrew Robinson.

It was staged in the echoing emptiness of BT's television studio in East London and lasted just 88 seconds. If Williams was irritated by the appalling pre-fight pronunciation of "Clydach Vale" by Warren's American MC, it was nothing to his ire when a clash of skulls left him bleeding from the hairline. He stormed in with both fists, driving the Redditch man around the ring before digging a left beneath the ribs which had the bewildered challenger failing to beat the count.

Within days the winner had surrendered his position, enabling Warren to have a proposed eliminator involving his fighter, Denzel Bentley, upgraded to a full title fight, while negotiators went ahead for the showdown with Andrade. The deal included a promise that Williams would be given a crack at his old post should he fall short of his world dream.

It remains to be seen whether he will take up the offer or focus on earning another bid for global glory. Meanwhile his disappointment has been eased by the arrival of a son, Oscar, whose name will no doubt join that of his half-sister, Myla, on the trunks the next time their father climbs through the ropes.

THE SUPPORTING CAST

The champions and challengers have, inevitably, taken pride of place in these pages. But there are many others who have, in a variety of ways, contributed to the rich tapestry of Rhondda boxing.

They date back to the beginning, with the bareknuckle brigade who earned fame – or, in some cases, notoriety – such as the Ynyshir brothers, Sam and Ivor Thomas, who shared the nickname 'Butcher', and Jack Northey, from Ystrad, a hot-headed individual who eventually suffered the fate of all ageing gunslingers when he refused to accept the challenge of a couple of young bucks and was given a good kicking as a result.

There was the fearsome mountain fighter, Lewis Roderick, whose wrists were too big to fit into the police handcuffs on the many occasions the boys in blue came calling.

Another in constant bother with the law was Ferndale fighter Gomer Perkins, regularly collared for collecting bets on street corners. He became the subject of a cause célèbre when, while serving a jail sentence for perjury, he was certified insane and transferred to an asylum in Bridgend. Public meetings in protest led to an 11,000-signature petition to the Home Secretary before he was eventually released without explanation.

But the Old Bill themselves had some useful boxers, including Will Cummins, a Welsh ABA champion in 1914, who captained Treorchy RFC and picked up four Wales caps as a No 8 in 1922.

More than a century after the sinking of the *Titanic*, let us recall the two valley boys who were lost with her. Dai Bowen, from Treherbert, and Les Williams, from Tonypandy, were sailing to the US to box for a Pittsburgh promoter. Ironically, they were supposed to travel a few days earlier, but delayed their departures to have new suits made. Bowen wrote, poignantly, to his mother: "This is a lovely boat, she is very near so big as Treherbert..."

Another lost too soon was Tonypandy's Emlyn Jones, cousin of legendary Wales fly-half Cliff Jones, who moved to Surrey and, having won a string of titles as a junior, lost only three of his 23 pro bouts in the immediate postwar years before dying of bone cancer

Emlyn Jones, cousin of fly-half star Cliff

Two Rhondda boxers were lost with the Titanic

at just 19. Other youngsters made their own decisions to leave us wondering how good they might have been, notably two Gilfach Goch products, Gareth Lawrence and Russell Rees.

Lawrence, the first Welsh boxer to claim four British schoolboy titles, had won all eight as a pro when he opted to turn his back on the sport, while Rees, alias 'Ducky', had six straight successes when he called it a day, before returning, six years later, for the shortest comeback in history. It consisted of just one punch, which was enough to halt Plymouth's Des Sowden in 10 seconds. Neither victor nor vanquished ever boxed again.

More recently, repeated eye problems forced premature retirement on Alex Hughes, from Maerdy, a British champion at schools, junior and youth level who went on to win his first 13 paid bouts – the last four successes all coming in the first round – before doctors shattered his dreams.

The heroism of the ring was often reflected in wider struggles, as exemplified by two sons of Treherbert.

Welterweight Dai Davies, known as 'Dai Chips', once captured five Germans single-handedly during World War I. On another occasion he and a comrade went into battle armed only with shovels, before a shrapnel wound brought an early end to his crazy gallantry.

Lightweight Tom Picton, mentioned in dispatches for his bravery as a naval stoker in that conflict, set off two decades later to fight Fascism in the Spanish Civil War, only to be wounded and later captured by Franco's troops. When he saw a prison guard batter another inmate with his rifle butt, Tom flattened the assailant with his bare fists. He was promptly thrown against a wall and shot dead.

Boxing is often a family matter and the Rhondda is no exception. As well as the Johns and Joneses profiled earlier, there were four Enochs, farmer's sons from Tonyrefail, five Norris brothers from Blaenclydach – Tom claimed the Welsh heavy crown in the 1920s – and another four Lewises, from Stanleytown. The youngest, Dickie Lewis, who challenged for the Welsh fly belt, had both legs broken as a five-year-old, when a shed collapsed; the playmate who went for help was Elfed Davies, later MP for Rhondda East.

There are also the fathers and sons, epitomised by Penygraig flyweight Bryn Griffiths, a Commonwealth Games rep who went on to box professionally, and his dad, Tommy, known as 'Darkie', a decent featherweight and former prisoner-of-war who was a regular at ex-boxers' events right up to his death in 2015 at the age of 95.

Others have earned respect for their services outside the ropes. Journalist Emlyn Michael, originally from Clydach Vale, was secretary of the Welsh Board of Control in its early days and also played a huge part in raising funds for hospitals. He was just 39 when he died at his Penygraig home.

On the promotional side, the man who kept Rhondda boxing alive in the years after World War II was Albert Davies, from Trealaw, who staged a series of shows at the local Judge's Hall as well as other valley venues, featuring many of Tommy Farr's comeback fights. Davies, who had a flourishing electrical business, later emigrated and died in Australia at the age of 77.

Gareth Lawrence – should have been a champion

Bryn Griffiths and his Dad, Tommy

Promoter Albert Davies

Pentre's Tony Wynne, a Welsh ABA champion back in 1967, is still active in his seventies as a referee and judge with the association and the unpaid code has seen other Rhondda men write footnotes in history.

Frank Salmon, an amateur from Ynyshir, claimed to have taken part in the first boxing to be televised – an exhibition with Ernie Kemp at the BBC studio at Alexandra Palace in early 1936, broadcast to a public audience as part of the experimental period before the service was officially launched. Based in London, Salmon boxed for England and Britain, but never for Wales – there were no expenses paid and he couldn't afford the train fare.

And Kerry Webber, from Gilfach Goch, was influential in prompting the Commonwealth Games to change its rules. He benefited from the last ditch call-up of Welsh boxers to fill the gaps in the 1986 competition in Edinburgh, following an anti-apartheid boycott. Webber, known as 'Pepe', was stopped in just 21 seconds by one of the few Africans left, Swaziland's Leonard Makhanya, but still received a bronze. Ever since, a boxer has had to achieve at least one victory before a medal can be awarded.

The conveyor belt is still producing new talent to follow in the bootsteps of those remembered here. Redhead Jordan Withers, from Ystrad, is a former GB youth champion now setting out on a pro career he hopes will prove that his label as "the Welsh Canelo" is based on more than his colouring.

One amateur who went on to write about the sport was Blaencwm-born Ron Berry, whose novel *So Long, Hector Bebb* tells of a Rhondda boxer's fight to survive.

But no author would dare dream up the bizarre ending to a bout at Treherbert in 1920. When Moses Davies and Young Attwood were entangled on the ropes, Davies pulled his arm back to deliver a blow and contrived to elbow himself in the unmentionables. He was in such agony that his seconds, presumably stifling their laughter, threw in the towel.

BIBLIOGRAPHY

The following are among many publications consulted during the writing of this book:

Sporting Life, Mirror of Life, Boxing, Boxing News, Boxing Monthly, Western Mail, South Wales Echo, South Wales Daily News, Merthyr Express, Aberdare Leader, Pontypridd Observer, Rhondda Leader.
Wales and its Boxers, ed. Peter Stead and Gareth Williams (University of Wales)
Fighting was my Business, by Jimmy Wilde (Robson)
Thus Farr, by Tommy Farr (Optomen)
A Welshman in the Bronx, by Graeme Kent (Gomer)
Man of Courage, by Bob Lonkhurst (Book Guild)
All in my Corner, by Tony Lee (TL Associates)
For the Love of the Game, by Vernon Ball (Tempus)
Welsh Boxing Annual 2019/20, by Dewi Powell (Powell)

The following websites were also useful sources of information:

Boxrec.com, Welsh Warriors, www.boxinghistory.org.uk, Amateur Boxing Results, Rootschat, Rootsweb, Ancestry, Find My Past.

St David's Press

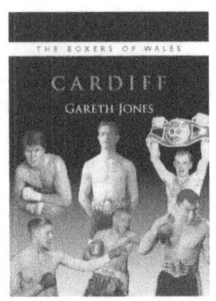

THE BOXERS OF WALES
CARDIFF

'Some of the greatest boxers in Britain have come out of Cardiff and this book is a must read for fight fans, whether you're Welsh or not.'
    Colin Hart, *The Sun*

'This book is not just about the famous fighters, it's about the forgotten heroes.'
    Steve Bunce, Boxing Broadcaster & Journalist

'A compelling and fascinating study.'
    Claude Abrams, Editor, *Boxing News*

978-1-902719-26-9   160pp   £14.99   PB

THE BOXERS OF WALES
MERTHYR
ABERDARE & PONTYPRIDD

'a masterpiece... a must-read for any boxing fan...Compelling stuff.'
    Steve Lillis, *News of the World*

'The valleys of south Wales have produced many fighters known worldwide ... but this book reminds us that there were others who lit up the ring in their day.'
    Gareth A. Davies, *Daily Telegraph*

978-1-902719-29-0   160pp   £14.99   PB

THE BOXERS OF WALES
SWANSEA & LLANELLI

'My co-commentator, Enzo Maccarinelli, keeps telling me what a great fight town Swansea is. And here's the evidence. It's not just about the big names, like Colin Jones, Ronnie James and the Curvises - here you can learn of the only Welsh-speaker ever to win a Scottish title and the Llanelli girl who took on Germany's boxing queen. A great read!'
    John Rawling, Commentator, *BoxNation*

'This book is a must for all serious boxing fans.'
    Graham Houston, Editor, *Boxing Monthly*

978-1-902719-450   176pp   £14.99   PB

THE BOXERS OF WALES
NEWPORT
THE GWENT VALLEYS AND MONMOUTHSHIRE

'Nobody knows Welsh boxing with quite the depth, understanding and empathy of Gareth Jones.'
    Kevin Mitchell, *The Observer*

'Gareth Jones is THE authority on Welsh boxing, and always a joy to read. His exhaustive research uncovers wonderful stories that should not be missed.'
    Matt Christie, Editor, *Boxing News*

978-1-902719-634   192pp   £14.99   PB

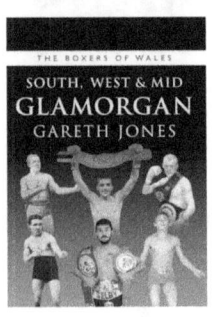

THE BOXERS OF WALES
SOUTH, WEST & MID
GLAMORGAN

'The Selby boys are here. Amateur glory, world title, so much talent. But once again it is a fighter that only the purest of fans can recall who catches the eye. This time it is Wee Willie Davies, a world-class flyweight, born near Maesteg, who moved to America as a child and met nine world champions. Welsh boxing, British boxing and even world boxing owes Gareth a great debt.'
    Steve Bunce

978-1-902719-801   176pp   £16.99   PB

www.ingramcontent.com/pod-product-compliance
Lightning Source LLC
Chambersburg PA
CBHW080735230426
43665CB00020B/2747